THE LATER YEARS OF
CHILDBEARING

This is the third and final report on the Princeton Fertility Study

The first two are

Family Growth in Metropolitan America, by Charles F. Westoff, Robert G. Potter, Jr., Philip C. Sagi, and Elliot G. Mishler

The Third Child: A Study in the Prediction of Fertility, by Charles F. Westoff, Robert G. Potter, Jr., and Philip C. Sagi

PUBLISHED FOR THE OFFICE OF POPULATION RESEARCH

PRINCETON UNIVERSITY

THE LATER YEARS OF CHILDBEARING

Larry L. Bumpass
and
Charles F. Westoff

PRINCETON UNIVERSITY PRESS

PRINCETON, NEW JERSEY

1970

Publication of this book has been aided by
the Office of Population Research, Princeton
University

This book has been composed in Linotype Caledonia
Printed in the United States of America
by Princeton University Press

Foreword

It is a special privilege to be invited to write the Foreword to this third and final volume of the Princeton Fertility Study. The book brings to conclusion a project launched 16 years ago under the guidance of a Steering Committee on which I served as Chairman. The occasion is one for extending the warmest congratulations to the staff of the study, to their colleagues in the Office of Population Research, and to the financial sponsors of the project.

Above all, special thanks are due to Professor Charles F. Westoff, who has been the driving spirit behind the project for the full 16 years of its life. It is very largely due to his efforts that this project, one of the longest sustained investigations in the social science field, has been carried to its distinguished completion in accordance with the original plans. The work has brought wholly new dimensions to the study of human fertility and has gone far toward freeing such study from dependence on cross-sectional data for the support of longitudinal inferences.

This study, in turn, grew out of the Indianapolis Study of Social and Psychological Factors Affecting Fertility, on which work began in 1938 under the sponsorship of the Milbank Memorial Fund and the editorship of P. K. Whelpton and Clyde V. Kiser. What is less generally known is that both sets of studies were undertaken mainly because Frederick Osborn kept prodding his demographic friends at the Scripps Foundation, the Milbank Memorial Fund, and the Office of Population Research to lay the plans. He then turned his attention toward helping to raise the needed funds.

Although this volume ends the Princeton Fertility Study, it too has a successor in the National Fertility Study being conducted by Professor Charles F. Westoff and Professor Norman B. Ryder (of the University of Wisconsin) under contract with the National Institute of Child Health and Human Development. The second round of field work for

v

that study is now being planned. Thus, the present book is the last of the second generation in a family of studies begun in 1938 and still developing vigorously.

All of this would have been quite impossible without financial support from the Carnegie Corporation, and both technical and financial support from the Milbank Memorial Fund and the Population Council. Most important of all was the assistance of the Office of Population Research which, under the direction of Professor Ansley J. Coale, has provided both professional assistance and the institutional base. To all of these, on behalf of the original Steering Committee, I give our warmest congratulations and heartfelt thanks.

FRANK W. NOTESTEIN
Visiting Senior Research Demographer
Office of Population Research
Princeton University

Preface

In the course of the 16 years or so between the initial planning of this study and the publication of the final volume in the series, a considerable number of people contributed along the way. In the early days of the Study we relied upon a Steering Committee composed of Chairman Frank W. Notestein, Ansley J. Coale, Ronald Freedman, Philip M. Hauser, Dudley Kirk, Clyde V. Kiser, Frank Lorimer, Donald G. Marquis, Frederick Osborn, Lowell J. Reed, and P. K. Whelpton. Elliot G. Mishler participated actively in the first phase, and Robert G. Potter and Philip C. Sagi devoted quite a few years to this research during both the first and second phases.

The fieldwork for all three phases of the research was carried out by National Analysts, Inc., of Philadelphia. During the last years of the study we relied principally on Aaron Spector who is now the Director of the Institute for Survey Research at Temple University.

A special word of appreciation is due Hazel Chafey of the Office of Population Research who assumed responsibility for keeping track of the whereabouts of our sample for some 8 years. Thanks are also due Frances Colwell and Anne Ryder of the Office for their secretarial services.

These years have witnessed radical change in data processing technology from simple card sorting equipment to giant computers. Different persons participated at various stages of this development: Erna Härm, Wanda Pieslak, Sherrill Buhler, and Greta Shapiro.

In the final analysis our thanks must be extended to all of the women in our sample who were interviewed but especially to the 814 who were generous enough to participate in all three interviews.

Contents

List of Tables

xiii

THE LATER YEARS OF
CHILDBEARING

I · Background, Sample, and Objectives

More than a dozen years ago—in the early months of 1957, to be precise—we talked to a sample of mothers of two children in the first of a series of three interviews that was to span a decade. As the opening lines of the first volume reporting our early findings read: "This is a study of human fertility. Essentially it is a study of why American couples differ in the number of children they have."[1]

The present volume is our last report on the fertility of these women as they near the end of their reproductive lives. It encompasses the results of our third and final round of interviews and exploits the longitudinal design of the study to learn how well attitudes and events of the early years of marriage determine the record of the later years of childbearing. How well are couples able to predict their own fertility over the years? How stable are women's family-size preferences over a decade? To what extent does the number of children desired affect the spacing of births? How much does the effectiveness of contraceptive practice in the later years of marriage depend on the number of children desired? What is the nature of the effects of religion on these processes? How is fertility affected by peer group relations, by the wife's participation in the labor force, by the sex of offspring at different stages of family growth, by personality characteristics? What are the interrelations of fertility and socioeconomic mobility?

These are the main questions posed in this report. The emphasis is on fertility viewed as a process developing through time, a system in which the final state is in part determined by events and "states" defined at early stages and in part affected by redefinitions and reevaluations as the process unfolds. This notion of feedback—that fertility affects fertility—can be quickly illustrated by the simple though not unimportant example of the effects of sex dis-

[1] Charles F. Westoff, Robert G. Potter, Philip C. Sagi and Elliot G. Mishler, *Family Growth in Metropolitan America* (Princeton: Princeton University Press, 1961), p. 5.

3

tribution on family size. Although a couple may be generally aiming for a family of three children, their family-size objectives are likely to be modified if the three children are all of the same sex.

Research Tradition

The recent history of survey research on American fertility can be seen as two parallel and functionally related streams. The first is represented by the Growth of American Family (GAF) studies conducted in 1955[2] and 1960,[3] continued in 1965 as the National Fertility Study,[4] and planned for 1970 by the same group. These studies were initially concerned with estimating certain parameters of interest such as the proportion of women in the United States who were sterile, using some method of contraception, or the like. Unlike official data collected by government agencies, these private surveys could provide information on such "sensitive" topics as these and include cross-tabulations with characteristics such as religion that still remain beyond the politically tolerable range of government data collection activities. The researchers in the early GAF studies were also interested in the collection of data on the number of children expected in order to facilitate the construction of population forecasts, an objective abandoned in the more recent studies.[5] In general, these studies have been less concerned with hypothesis testing than with exploring and describing the fertility behavior and attitudes of American couples.

The other research tradition, represented chiefly by the present Princeton Fertility Study and the Detroit Area

[2] Ronald Freedman, Pascal K. Whelpton, and Arthur A. Campbell, *Family Planning, Sterility and Population Growth* (New York: McGraw Hill, 1959).

[3] Pascal K. Whelpton, Arthur A. Campbell, and John E. Patterson, *Fertility and Family Planning in the United States* (Princeton: Princeton University Press, 1966).

[4] Norman B. Ryder and Charles F. Westoff, *Reproduction in the United States: 1965* (Princeton: Princeton University Press, in press).

[5] See Norman B. Ryder and Charles F. Westoff, "The Trend of Expected Parity in the United States: 1955, 1960, 1965," *Population Index*, 33, No. 2 (1967): 153-68.

Study,[6] has focused more on the testing of various hypotheses about the fertility process and its determinants in highly specialized samples. This stream of research is descended more directly from the Indianapolis Study of Social Psychological Factors Affecting Fertility,[7] the first major private study of fertility in this country if not in the world. Planned originally as an effort to go beyond the routine kinds of statistics published by the government in order to probe the social and psychological structure of fertility, the Indianapolis Study bequeathed a rich heritage of findings, new hypotheses, and methodological experience as well as a number of social scientists trained in this type of research. When the Princeton Fertility Study was conceived, its theoretical organization and substance were drawn almost exclusively from the Indianapolis Study; its longitudinal and sample designs were direct results of elaborate self-criticism by the researchers in that study. This criticism and the rationale for the resulting decisions have been described in the opening chapter of the first volume of the Princeton Study. Here we shall review our basic study and sample design only briefly, concentrating more on the details of the third and final round of interviews on which the present volume is based.

The Study Design

One repeated criticism of the Indianapolis Study, and a recurrent problem in most current fertility research, has been that data collected in a single cross-sectional survey

[6] Reports based on this study include Ronald Freedman, Lolagene Coombs, and Larry Bumpass, "Stability and Change in Expectations about Family Size: a Longitudinal Study," *Demography* 2 (1965): 250-75; Ronald Freedman, Lolagene Coombs, and Judith Friedman, "Social Correlates of Fetal Mortality," *Milbank Memorial Fund Quarterly* 44, No. 3 (1966): 327-44; Ronald Freedman and Lolagene Coombs, "Childspacing and Family Economic Position," *American Sociological Review* 31, No. 5 (1966), 631-48; and Larry Bumpass, "Stability and Change in Family Size Expectations over the First Two Years of Marriage," *Journal of Social Issues* 23, No. 4 (1967): 83-98.

[7] Pascal K. Whelpton and Clyde V. Kiser, eds., *Social and Psychological Factors Affecting Fertility* (New York: Milbank Memorial Fund, 5 vols., 1946, 1950, 1952, 1954, and 1958).

are of limited value because respondents are required to recollect events long past. In addition to simple memory difficulties, such recall is vulnerable to all of the subtle processes of *post factum* rationalization of events of critical importance to the demographer, such as whether a pregnancy was planned. Aside from such problems of measurement reliability (see Chapter VIII for an empirical assessment of the reliability of such information), there is the difficulty of disentangling the temporal sequence of events. A case in point is the relationship between the number of children desired and achieved fertility (see Chapter IV). In a cross-sectional survey the two variables are measured simultaneously and there is an obvious opportunity for contamination, that is, for the number desired to be adjusted to the reality of the number achieved.

It was against a background of such considerations that a longitudinal research design was selected. We decided to interview a group of women beginning at a common point in their fertility history and follow them through to the end of their reproductive careers.

The definition of the starting point was problematic. Logically it would have been desirable to begin with a cohort of couples just entering marriage and follow them until the women completed menopause. But even aside from the not inconsiderable fact that such research would imply a commitment of some 25 years, there are the practical difficulties of following young people who tend to be extremely mobile in the early years of married life. Moreover almost all couples have at least one child and a very high proportion of those with one go on to have a second. We therefore decided to begin our study with a sample of couples with two children, all of whom had experienced their second birth at the same time (this worked out fortuitously to September 1956). Instead of an age or marriage cohort, we had substituted the idea of a parity cohort; all women shared the fact of having given birth to their second child at the same time. At the time we were also interested in studying couples actively participating in the

6

baby boom of the 1950's; having a second child in 1956 placed these couples squarely in the stream of this period.

The Sample Design

The primary objective of the sample design was to represent couples with two children whose second birth occurred in September 1956. The ordinary survey research procedures of knocking on doors of randomly selected dwelling units was obviously impracticable since the ratio of eligible couples to the general population was in the order of 1 to 4,000. Fortunately we were able to secure the cooperation of the Office of Vital Statistics in the areas sampled to provide us with a sampling frame; otherwise the study as designed would have been quite impossible.

Eligibility for inclusion involved several criteria. We decided to restrict the sample to the largest metropolitan areas of the country—those with populations of at least 2,000,000 persons. Our area of interest was thus defined to include[8] the Standard Metropolitan Areas of New York, Chicago, Los Angeles, Philadelphia, Detroit, San Francisco–Oakland, and Pittsburgh. This decision, as most such decisions, was prompted by budgetary considerations; it would have been prohibitively expensive to draw a national sample. A sample that included large urban and suburban populations, one in which persons of all religions would be adequately represented, seemed to be the best compromise.

We also had to restrict the sample to native-born, white couples for the same reason. Since ethnic subcultures require separate analyses in the study of fertility, we could not have afforded a sufficiently large sample to make such analyses feasible. Still other restrictions were imposed to facilitate analysis from a sample of limited size. We eliminated couples who were married more than once, who had been separated, or whose fertility history was complicated by child mortality, extensive pregnancy wastage, plural

[8] Boston—the one city of this size not included—had to be excluded because the information assembled in the Vital Statistics Office did not contain birth order.

births, adoption, or current pregnancy. In connection with pregnancy wastage, the criterion of a maximum of one miscarriage was established.

The general aim was to interview a sample of women from the mainstream of American life whose reproductive life, at least up to the time of the second birth, was largely free of complicating factors. Although these restrictions operated to make the population sampled a fairly specialized one, they also served to define a set of subjects who were ideally refined for analytical purposes.

In sum then, the sample initially selected represents native-born, white married couples, resident in the nation's largest metropolitan areas, who had recently had a second child and whose marital and pregnancy histories were uncomplicated.

The target sample size was 1,150 couples—a number arrived at through consideration of the size of the smallest subgroup deemed necessary for analysis. On the basis of pretest experiences which helped to determine the eligibility rates, a simple random sample was drawn from the punchcard records of the relevant Vital Statistics Offices.

The First Interview: 1957

The interviews were conducted between 4 and 6 months after the month of birth of the second child—an interval selected to maximize the psychological distance from the event of that birth while simultaneously minimizing the probability of another pregnancy. National Analysts, Inc., of Philadelphia was chosen to provide the interviewing staff, coding and card punching services. We organized two three-day training sessions for these interviewers (who were typically middle-aged married women who had worked on numerous other consumer surveys) in which they were informed about the purposes of the research and instructed in the myriad details of the interview schedule (a similar training school was established for each of the two subsequent interviews as well).

The interview schedules designed for each of the three

8

interviews were quite similar,[9] but the first was the longest, requiring an hour and a half on the average to administer. In addition at the first interview, two self-administered mail questionnaires were left with the respondent—a personality inventory for her to complete and a questionnaire for her husband to complete on attitudes toward work. Both of these were returned by mail with a gratifyingly high response rate (over 80 percent in both cases). The response rate on the primary interview was excellent. A total of 1,165 interviews were completed—a completion rate of 88.7 percent (see Table 1).[10]

Table 1. Field results of the three interviews of the Princeton Fertility Study

	1957 First interview		1960 Second interview		1963-67 Third interview	
Outcome	N	Percent	N	Percent	N	Percent
Ineligible[a] or deceased	395		36		35	
Eligible	1314	100.0	1129	100.0	870	100.0
Completed	1165	88.7	905	80.2	814	93.6
Refusal	83	6.3	92	8.1	41	4.7
Moved, no address	---	---	95	8.4	9	1.0
Not at home or unable to contact or locate	53	4.0	30	2.6	4	.4
Ill or other	13	1.0	7	.6	2	.2

[a]For first interview includes those who had moved out of the Metropolitan Areas by the time of survey.

[9] See Appendix A in Charles F. Westoff, Robert G. Potter, and Philip C. Sagi, *The Third Child* (Princeton: Princeton University Press, 1963) for the heart of the interview schedule.
[10] The full details are available in Chapters 1-2 of Westoff, Potter, Sagi and Mishler, *Family Growth in Metropolitan America.*

9

The Second Interview: 1960

The analysis of data collected in the first interview in 1957, reported in *Family Growth in Metropolitan America,* focused on the determinants and interrelations of the number of children desired (as measured 4 to 6 months after the birth of the second child), the length of the interval between marriage and the second birth, and the success with which the couple had planned their fertility thus far.

The second interview was scheduled in 1960, 3 years after the first contact. The reason for this timing was to maximize the proportion of third births that would have occurred while keeping to a minimum the percentage who would have had a fourth birth. (A total of 46 percent had no pregnancy during the interval, 43 percent reported one, and 11 percent reported two pregnancies.) The analysis of these data, reported in *The Third Child,* concentrated on explaining the fertility experience during that 3-year period: whether or not the couple had a third child, if so the interval of time elapsed, and the success in controlling fertility during the interval. More generally, the central theoretical concern was the extent to which the number and spacing of births reflect explicit preferences rather than accidental factors such as contraceptive failure, pregnancy wastage, or slowness to conceive—a theme that guides much of the analysis in the present volume as well.

The objective of the field work in the second round of interviews was to interview every woman still eligible; women were considered ineligible if they had been widowed, divorced, or permanently separated from their husbands. In addition a small number of wives (13) who reported at the first interview having had a sterilizing operation were not reinterviewed.

The results of the 1960 effort were less satisfactory mainly because we were inexperienced in the techniques of tracking respondents who had moved. The refusal rate was also higher the second time. Of the original sample of 1,165 of whom 1,129 were not known to be ineligible, interviews were completed successfully with 905 for a completion rate of 80.2 percent (Table 1). An analysis of the biases introduced by this attrition revealed that at the time of the first interview the 905 couples had higher income and more education, and included disproportionately more Jews, fewer Catholics, and a slightly higher proportion of successful family planners than the remainder. They did not differ significantly on number of children desired, interval between marriage and second birth, and numerous other characteristics of interest. Perhaps more importantly there are very few differences of any magnitude in the correlations between variables in the samples interviewed in 1957 and 1960.

The Third Interview: 1963-67

The main objective of the third and last interview was to determine the number of children that our panel of couples would have by the end of their reproductive years. Ideally, this would mean waiting until the fact of menopause was clearly established. Such delay was impractical, unnecessary, and in some respects even undesirable. It was impractical because it would have delayed the last interview perhaps as long as 10 more years. It was unnecessary because we know enough about the age distribution of marital fertility to realize that the vast majority of women have had their last child before age 40 (95 percent) and that even 73 percent have completed their fertility by age 35.[11] And finally it would have been undesirable to delay the final interview until the biological termination of fertility because it would have meant increasing greatly the risks of sample attrition and reducing the quality of retrospective data.

In view of the fact that the age of our respondents varied considerably at the birth of their second child (with a mean of 27 and a standard deviation of 4.5), a plan was

[11] Based on the experience of white women born 1910-19, U.S. Bureau of the Census, *Current Population Reports*, Series P-20, No. 108, Table 13.

evolved to spread the last series of interviews out over a period of time and phase the sample out beginning with a group of women who were at least 36.5 years of age, had been married at least 11 years, and who did not intend to have any additional children. We divided the sample into five such groups and interviewed them over the 5-year period from 1963 through 1967. In the last year, 1967, we interviewed the women in our sample who according to information collected at the second interview in 1960 had the most incomplete fertility records (young women who wanted the largest number of additional children). Characteristics of these five groups at the time of the third interview are shown in Table 2.

Table 2. Characteristics of the third interview respondents, by year of third interview

| Characteristic | Year of interview | | | | | |
	63	64	65	66	67	Total
Wife's age	40.1	36.5	35.7	33.9	33.0	35.6
Years since marriage	15.1	14.4	14.0	12.8	14.2	14.2
Years since last birth	5.4	5.5	5.3	4.7	5.7	5.4
Percent of expected already born	99	99	98	97	97	98
Number of respondents	138	168	152	133	233	814

While this interviewing design maximizes completed fertility and minimizes sample attrition it also introduces some methodological difficulties. Different lengths of time have elapsed between interviews which means that individuals interviewed over the 5 years have been exposed to different amounts of time and experience; and these differences are by design associated with age and fertility. This factor is

12

most problematic with respect to life-cycle variables such as status mobility (for a discussion of its implications in this context see Chapter VII). In general this appears not to be a serious problem.

Of the 905 women interviewed for the second time in 1960, 35 were ineligible for the third interview, leaving a target of 870 to be interviewed for the last time. We were able to successfully complete interviews with 814 or 93.6 percent, a very satisfactory completion rate. The bulk of the nonrespondents refused to be interviewed again (see Table 1); only 13 were "lost" because of failures to locate the family.[12]

The 814 are a very representative subsample of the 1,165 couples initially interviewed back in 1957. Comparing the 814 with the 1,094 couples who would still have presumably been eligible for the third interview—a procedure that may overestimate the differences[13]—produces a number of statistically significant differences between respondents and nonrespondents (Table 3). The differences tend to represent the same biases that characterized the attrition from the first to the second interview. Those interviewed in the third round by comparison with the initial sample tend to be somewhat older, drawn from a higher socioeconomic status, composed of more Jews and fewer Catholics than expected, and are slightly more likely to have

[12] This considerable accomplishment resulted from the assiduous efforts of Mrs. Hazel Chafey of the Office of Population Research, Princeton University, whose responsibility it was to maintain an annual check on the addresses of each couple in the sample until they were interviewed. A battery of techniques was employed. The first and main technique was to check the address through the telephone directories. If that failed or indicated a move, a request for change of address information was filed with the Post Office. If both of these failed, other approaches were brought into play including letters or telephone calls to the relatives or friends whose names and addresses had been supplied to us in 1960 for precisely this reason, checks with neighbors by interviewers in the area, and finally, if all else failed, the services of the Retail Credit Bureau were employed.

[13] Some fraction of those who were never located or who refused to be interviewed were undoubtedly ineligible and theoretically should be excluded from this comparison.

13

Table 3. Differences between the original and final samples on selected characteristics

| Characteristic | Value in 1957 | | Significance level of the difference between respondents and nonrespondents |
	Original sample[a] N = 1,094	Final sample N = 814	
Mean number of children desired	3.3	3.3	NS
Percent successful or semi-successful planners	60	61	NS
Mean interval from marriage to second birth	5.0	5.1	NS
Mean age of wife	27.2	27.4	.01
Mean age of husband	29.5	29.7	.02
Mean age of wife at marriage	21.5	21.7	.001
Percent Protestant	39	41	NS
Percent Catholic	50	47	.01
Percent Jewish	11	12	.05
Mean years of wife's education	12.3	12.5	.001
Mean years of husband's education	12.6	12.8	.001
Mean 1956 income	$5362	$5790	.001
Percent white-collar class	50	53	.01
Mean number of moves since marriage	2.5	2.5	NS

[a]Excluding 71 couples known to be ineligible for subsequent interviews.

planned their fertility successfully. However the effect of
these differences on the final sample is of little substantive
importance.

Again, since this study is focused more on analytical
questions than on estimates of particular parameters, the

critical question seems to be less whether the two samples differ slightly on this or that characteristic but more whether the interrelations among variables in the final sample are what might be expected if there had been no attrition. Some estimate of this can be gained by comparing the matrix of intercorrelations among the major variables derived from the primary sample with the same matrix based on the final sample. As in the earlier comparisons of univariate distributions, this comparison is based on the initial sample (1,165) excluding those 71 couples known to be ineligible for subsequent interviews. In Table 4 we show

Table 4. Comparison between intercorrelations among 31 major variables for the first[a] and third panels

Absolute differences	Number of differences	Percent	Cumulative percent
Total	465	100.0	100.0
.00	96	20.6	100.0
.01	154	33.1	79.3
.02	115	24.7	46.2
.03	66	14.2	21.5
.04	21	4.5	7.3
.05	9	1.9	2.8
.06	4	.9	.9

[a]Excluding 71 couples known to be ineligible for subsequent interviews.

the distribution of differences between each of the 465 correlations computed on the two samples. It is quite clear that the overwhelming proportion of these differences are trivial; nearly four-fifths of all differences are .02 or less, and less than 1 percent reach a difference of .06.

It would seem reasonable to conclude from this analysis that the failure to include some of our respondents in the

15

final re-interview has not greatly affected our ability to generalize. Of course the ultimate population of interest is the one from which the primary sample was drawn which was subject to sampling error as well as refusals to be interviewed, inability to locate respondents, and so forth. The attrition in subsequent interviews can be regarded as an extension of this original departure from representativeness.

Organization of this Volume

The analysis of data collected in the third interview and reported in this volume concentrates on the exploitation of the longitudinal design in which fertility is viewed as a process unfolding over time. The next chapter (II) focuses on the assessment of the stability of the number of children desired as reported initially after the birth of the second child and again toward the end of the reproductive years. The amount of stability is examined at both the aggregate and individual levels. One of the difficult analytical questions covered in this chapter is the evaluation of how much of the change results from instability and how much from unreliability of measurement.

In Chapter III a model is developed in which preferences for the timing of births are viewed as related more to the total span of child care as determined by the total number of children desired than to the length of specific intervals. The general interest is in the factors associated with the timing of births.

How well completed family size can be predicted from desired family size and from other variables is the central concern of Chapter IV. Is the association between achieved and desired fertility greater in certain groups than in others; for example, do Protestants "predict" their completed fertility better than Catholics? Do women with more education reveal a higher correlation between what they want and what they do than women with less education? How much does the number of children desired by the husband add to the prediction of fertility? This chapter in some respects contains the core of the analysis of the theme that has dominated so much of our work: the extent to which fertility is determined by voluntary factors.

Chapter V renews an interest developed at length in the analysis of the second interview. The original interest in the mechanism of improvements in contraceptive effectiveness stemmed from the realization that if couples continued to experience during the later years of marriage contraceptive failures at the rate observed in the early years of childbearing, the number of children born would be considerably in excess of the actual number observed. Somehow or other, couples manage to improve radically their practice of contraception in the later childbearing years. The hypothesis originally developed and demonstrated in *The Third Child* that contraceptive effectiveness is a function of the achievement of desired family size is reexamined here in the light of 3 to 8 additional years of exposure toward the end of reproductive life.

The longitudinal design of this study covered the time period during which the oral contraceptive was marketed. Since questions to determine coital frequency were asked in both the second and third interviews, a "before and after" analysis was possible of the association between the pill and coital frequency—a subject about which there has been considerable speculation. This material is also reviewed in Chapter V.

Chapter VI concentrates on the influence of certain social and psychological factors on fertility. Again one focus is on change over time, for example, the effects of changes in religiousness over the years as measured by the frequency of attendance at religious services reported in different interviews. Other variables familiar to students of the subject include the wife's work history, the influence of the family size of friends and parents, the sex of offspring, and the battery of attitudinal and personality characteristics derived from the first interview in 1957.

Chapter VII is derived from research for a doctoral dissertation written by David Featherman at the University

17

of Michigan on the basis of data from this study.[14] Set in the framework of the classical social mobility hypothesis, the chapter considers fertility as a career contingency and finds no evidence that career mobility is impaired by high fertility; if anything, the data indicate a slight effect in the opposite direction.

The volume ends on a methodological note which exploits the longitudinal design to evaluate the reliability of retrospective data on fertility, contraception, and fertility-planning success. A considerable amount of unreliability in the measurement of critical variables is documented; this explains in part some of the consistently low correlations observed in such studies and underscores the great need for the improvement of measurement as one important and necessary path to the extension of scientific knowledge in this field.

[14] David L. Featherman, "The Socioeconomic Achievement of White Married Males in the United States 1957-67," Ph.D. dissertation, University of Michigan, 1969.

II · The Stability of Family-Size Desires

In spite of the secularization of the female role in our society, childrearing remains a most salient aspect of that role. Women still give ready answers when asked how many children they wish to have. But what is the nature of the replies to this question? Are family-size desires realistic assessments of the number of children women want to have, or are they merely reflections of what is perceived to be considered desirable by others? Are they thoughtful reactions or are they casual if not irresponsible responses to the fact that the question was asked?

Analyses reported elsewhere in this volume support the hypothesis that family-size desires at the achievement of second parity are meaningful goals for subsequent fertility-related behavior. In fact, second parity may represent an ideal point at which to measure family-size desires. Since there is a strong consensus that families ought to have at least two children, only after this minimum is achieved is it critical that desires crystallize to the extent of wanting an additional birth or not. This is not to assert that desired family size will not fluctuate after second parity for some couples in adjustment to changes in life circumstances. It does, however, imply that fertility-related behavior and completed family size will vary consistently with the number desired after the second birth. In this chapter we shall address the question of the stability and reliability of reports of family-size desires. The subject of the validity of family-size desires as predictors of actual fertility is reviewed in Chapter IV.

A Methodological Note

At the first interview women were asked, "How many children do you want to have *altogether*, counting the two you have now?" The same question was asked at the second interview with the substitution of "those" for "the two." However, at the third interview the question followed recall of the number desired after the second child was born and read, "At the present, how many more children, if any, would you like to have?"

This sequence of questions raises three problems for an analysis of the stability of family-size desires over time. On the one hand, the third interview question follows recall of the number desired at the time of the first interview. This factor might bias the results in the direction of stability insofar as respondents accurately remember the number they originally desired and strive to be consistent. On the other hand, the question asked at the third interview is not really the same question as that asked at the first. The fact that the first asks for a total number while the second asks for an additional number is probably inconsequential. But the transition from "do you want" to "would you like to have" injects a more conditional element into the third question that may introduce differences between the third and other responses which are not due to instability. A more serious problem results from the fact that none of these questions allows the option of desiring fewer children than current parity. This is fine for the prediction of fertility, since any less-than-parity desires would be unrealistic. But at the same time, this fact does not allow a woman who has exceeded her original desires to tell us whether she changed her mind or whether she had the additional birth in spite of the fact that her original desires remained unchanged. Somewhat as an artifact of the question design, then, all births in excess of first interview desires are rationalized upward as "changes" in the number of children desired.

Stability and Change of Family-Size Desires

Keeping in mind the above qualifications, several useful observations can be made about family-size desires as reported at the three interviews. We note in Table 5, a slight upward movement of family-size desires over this 8-year period. Since the mean number desired actually declined slightly between the first and second interviews, the up-

20

Table 5. Number of children desired as reported at the first, second and third interviews: 814 women

Interview	Total desired					Total percent	Mean
	2	3	4	5	6+		
First	30	31	31	4	3	100	3.3
Second	29	35	28	4	4	100	3.2
Third	27	35	21	9	8	100	3.4

ward shift after the second interview may well be tied to fertility in excess of that originally desired.

The general aggregate stability results from a large number of small but compensating changes on the part of individuals (Table 6). While two-fifths of the women give differing responses at the first and second interviews and nearly three-fifths give differing answers at the first and third interviews, the discrepancies are small. For the large majority of the women (approximately 85 percent) the

Table 6. Patterns of change in total number of children desired as reported at the first, second, and third interviews

Comparison	Changed up		No change	Changed down		Total percent	Net mean change
	2+	1		1	2+		
First and second interviews	4	16	59	19	3	100	-.1
Second and third interviews	7	20	54	12	7	100	.2
First and third interviews	10	25	42	20	4	100	.1

21

number desired at the third interview is within one child of the number desired at either the first or the second interview.

Again we see that net upward change occurs only between the second and third interviews when 9 percent more women changed up than changed down. Table 7 il-

Table 7. Change in number of children desired between first and third interviews, by comparison between number of children desired at first interview and completed fertility

	Comparison between first and third interview desires						
Comparison be-tween desires and fertility	Changed up		No change	Changed down		Total	
	2+	1		1	2+	Percent	N
Total	10	25	42	20	4	100	814
Fertility exceeds desires by:							
2 +	91	8	1	-	-	100	65
1	6	91	3	-	-	100	176
Fertility same as desires	3	10	87	-	-	100	332
Fertility less than desires by:							
1	-	2	16	81	-	100	194
2 +	-	-	25	11	64	100	47

lustrates how closely changes in family-size desires are tied to fertility experience over these 8 years. The correlation between changes in fertility desires and whether fertility exceeded or was less than first interview desires is .89. Of course it is possible that changes in family-size desires preceded fertility, but it seems more likely that the temporal ordering may be the other way around for many women. Some 81 percent of the women who exceeded their original desires report their last pregnancy as unplanned. Thus much of what is recorded here as change in family-size desires may be unreliability in the reporting of these desires or, to put it another way, the *post factum* rationalization of unintended behavior.

Of course the effect of intervening fertility, or infertility, on the stability of family-size desires is contingent upon the number originally desired. Women desiring two children are susceptible only to upward change, but they are exposed over the complete study period to the risk of upward change due to an unwanted birth. On the other hand, women initially desiring large families may revise either upward or downward over much of the study period. Table 8 illustrates this dependence of stability on the num-

Table 8. Change in family-size desires between first and third interviews, by number desired at first interview

| Number desired at first interview | Comparison between first and third interview desires | | | | |
	Changed up	Stable	Changed down	Total Percent	N
2	45	55	-	100	240
3	32	41	26	100	256
4	29	32	39	100	248
5 +	24	28	48	100	58
Total	34	42	24	100	814

ber initially desired. Desires for two children are most stable but also most likely to revise upward, whereas desires for five or more children are least stable and most likely to revise downward.

23

With respect to the compensating nature of changes in family-size desires, very similar results were found among women in the Detroit Area Study over a 3-year period,[1] although "expected" number of children was employed in the Detroit Study while we are concerned here with "desired" number. (Analysis of the 1965 National Fertility Study demonstrates that these variables are distinguishable.[2]) When we compare the detailed patterns of change over three interviews, the similarities with the Detroit Area Study findings are striking (Table 9). In both studies, one-third of the women give exactly the same response at each of the three interviews, 4 percent change up in both intervals, and 3 percent change down in both intervals. Compensating changes on the part of the same women (up-down, down-up) are more prevalent in the Detroit Area Study, whereas a tendency for the changes of different women to be compensating is more evident in the Princeton data.

The Detroit Area Study records women's family-size orientations at one year intervals whereas the Princeton Study samples these orientations at intervals of three and five years. That the patterns of change should be so similar over such disparate intervals suggests something about the nature of family-size orientations. Such similarity would be expected under the conditions of high stability of desires but moderately high unreliability in the reporting of desires. If reports of family-size desires fluctuate randomly around rather stable values, then a cross-section at any point in time will find similar proportions of women reporting family-size desires discrepant with their "real" desires. As a consequence, comparisons between reports of family-size desires at different points in time might reveal similar patterns of discrepancy even though the intervals involved were dissimilar in length.

Heise has recently reported on a method of separating

---

[1] Freedman, Coombs, and Bumpass, "Stability and Change."

[2] Norman B. Ryder and Charles F. Westoff, "Relationships among Intended, Expected, Desired, and Ideal Family Size: United States, 1965," *Population Research* (March 1969).

Table 9. Combined pattern of .changes from first to second and second to third interviews: percent distributions for Princeton Fertility Study (PFS) 1957-67 and for the Detroit Area Study (DAS), 1962-63[a]

Change over three interviews	PFS	DAS
No change	32	34
Both changes down	3	3
Both changes up	4	4
Change down then up	7	11
Change up then down	5	10
Change down then stable	12	12
Change up then stable	10	10
Stable then down	11	7
Stable then up	15	9
Total:		
Percent	100	100
Number	814	1021

[a]Freedman, Coombs, and Bumpass, "Stability and Change," Table 3.

the elements of reliability and stability in variables measured in the same population at three points in time.[3] Through the introduction of the unmeasured "real" variable into a path-analytic framework, estimates can be made of the relationship between this unmeasured variable and the measured variable (reliability), and between the unmeasured variable at different points in time (stability). With reference to the Detroit Area Study data, Heise concluded:

[3] David R. Heise, "Separating Reliability and Stability in Test-Retest Correlation," *American Sociological Review* 34, No. 1 (1969): 93-101.

These reliability and stability coefficients suggest that a sizable proportion of the flux in family-size expectations is a matter of ambiguity in measurement rather than due to actual changes of mind.[4]

This conclusion is consistent with inferences made above, but there is some question as to the applicability of this method to family-size orientations because of the assumptions required by the path model. In particular, it is unlikely that these data meet the assumption that the correlation between the variable at the first and third points in time is mediated wholly through the correlations between times one and two, and times two and three (i.e., that the residuals are uncorrelated). It is very likely that background factors such as education have continued effects on fertility in addition to the effect mediated through initial desired family size. That such is the case, at least for some subgroups, is illustrated by the fact that among Jewish women family-size desires are more highly correlated between interviews one and three than between interviews one and two—with a resulting impossible estimate of over 1.0 for stability between the second and third interviews (Table 10). In addition, this model assumes that the unreliability component is the same at each measurement. If, as has been suggested, fertility is a major factor affecting the reliability of family-size desires as measured in this study, then the component of unreliability would be much greater at the third than at the first measurement because the third measure of desired family size would include a higher proportion of unwanted births.

Following Heise's procedure, estimates of stability and reliability have been made for the total sample and for religious and educational subgroups. Keeping in mind our reservations about the extent to which the assumptions of the procedure are met in these data, a number of interesting observations can be made from Table 10. The estimates of reliability and stability for family-size desires are lower

[4] *Ibid.*, 98.

Table 10. Estimates[a] of reliability and stability components of family-
size desires over the three interviews, by religion and
education, for both the Princeton Fertility Study and the
Detroit Area Study

Religion and education	Reliability	Stability			N
		1-2	2-3	1-3	
Detroit Area Study	.88	.81	.85	.78	1045
Princeton Fertility Study					
Total	.81	.87	.80	.69	814
Religion:					
Protestants	.76	.75	.84	.63	
Active	.71	.81	.91	.74	136
Other	.83	.66	.72	.47	197
Catholics	.80	.90	.73	.66	
Active	.98	.77	.61	.47	95
Other	.69	.95	.76	.73	288
Jews	.67	.92	1.03	.95	98
Education:					
Under 12 years	.73	.88	.82	.72	153
12 years	.82	.84	.78	.66	428
College	.83	.92	.82	.76	233

[a] See Heise: Reliability $= r_{12}r_{23}/r_{13}$; Stability 1-2 $= r_{13}/r_{23}$, 2-3 $= r_{13}/r_{12}$, 1-3 $= r_{13}^2/r_{23}$.

in these data than in the Detroit Area Study data, reflect-
ing perhaps the influences of the problematic factors discussed at the beginning of this chapter as well as the effect
of the longer interval. Differences by religion are quite
strong, with high reliability and low stability estimated for
Active Catholics,[5] and low reliability and high stability

[5] The designations "Active" and "Other" are explained at length
in Chapter VI.

estimated for Jewish women. Is this reasonable? Perhaps so, if intervening fertility is a major factor affecting reliability. Active Catholics, desiring large families, approach their desired family size only near the end of the study period. Consequently, there is little pressure from fertility in excess of desires to force the report of desires unreliably upward—the question design does not prohibit them from telling us exactly the number they want. Since at the birth of the second child completed family size is a more distant goal for these women, it may be less crystallized than it is for other women at this time and hence less stable. On the other hand, the opposite is true for Jewish women who, desiring small families, may be more certain of the number they want because they are closer to their goal at the first interview but who are simultaneously more exposed over the study period to changes in the report of desired number as a result of an unwanted birth. Most problematic is the fact that the estimates for Other Protestants resemble those for Active Catholics. If the above observations have any validity, different factors must underlie the high reliability and low stability observed for Other Protestants.

Respondents' education might be expected to relate to both reliability and stability. On the one hand, factors associated with reliability of reporting (including, for these measures, the prevention of unwanted births) may increase with the level of a respondent's education. On the other hand, stability of expectation may be higher for the more highly educated, in part because of the greater predictability of life circumstances. While both the reliability and the stability of family-size desires increase with education, the differences are small.

Summary and Conclusions

Aggregate stability over time in reports of family-size desires results from many small compensating changes on the part of individuals. Only one-third of the women give exactly the same response at each of the three interviews. On the other hand, for 85 percent the third response is within one child of the desired family size reported at the first interview. Is this high or low stability? In a population in which the standard deviation in completed family size is only 1.3, such instability in family-size desires might be considered too great for the variable to be of any value. If the number of children a woman wants to have fluctuates rapidly, it can hardly serve as a goal directing her family-planning behavior. However there have been several suggestions here that the measured instability in reports of number of children desired is more likely a product of unreliability than of instability in the unmeasured variable. Some of this unreliability is a result of the question design which prohibits a woman from reporting that although she has exceeded the number she originally desired, she would still like to have that original number. Changes in reports of desired family size are closely tied to fertility experience.

Reports of the number of children desired after the birth of the second child are least likely to be contaminated by these types of unreliability, and consequently should better represent long-term goals in terms of which family planning takes place. Much of what follows in this volume examines this hypothesis.

III · The Timing of Fertility

The timing of births is a critical dimension of fertility. Rates of population growth are closely tied to the average intervals between births and to changes in these intervals; from a sociological perspective, the time that a woman is involved in the intensive responsibilities of infant care, as well as the time when she will be largely freed of the mother role, is conditioned by how soon she starts her family and how closely she spaces her children.

We might expect a factor so directly related to female-role patterns to be an important component of family planning. This does not conflict with the assertion that contraception is more casual when spacing than when limiting births (supported in later chapters) since casual contraceptive practice is one way to realize desired short intervals. The notion that birth intervals are "planned" need not imply that women aim for intervals of a specific number of months; it may be that, in terms of their overall fertility plans, they seek intervals in loosely defined short or long ranges. In fact, the most salient dimensions of birth spacing may be the first birth interval and the interval between the first and last children, since these are the intervals determining the span of fertility within a woman's life cycle.

Reports of socioeconomic or religious differentials in birth spacing are usually set in the context of inferred preferences about birth intervals. How closely births ought to be spaced as well as the total number of children desired is seen as varying directly with subgroup emphasis on the mother role vis-à-vis other female roles. An alternative perspective is to view total family size and the span of fertility as the most salient aspects, with individual intervals largely a consequence of their interaction. The argument might be made that there is a vague but nonetheless real upper limit on what is considered a desirable span of intensive child care and that as a consequence women who

30

desire larger families must space their children more closely together. This model of interval planning does not assume that women have specific preferences about the interval length of any given order, but rather that the overall pace of family building responds to the size of the task undertaken and that the length of any specific interval may compensate for the lengths of earlier intervals.

Average Birth Intervals

Consistent with other evidence, average birth intervals experienced by the women in our sample are shortest for the first birth interval, about the same for the second and third births, and decline slightly for fourth and subsequent intervals. Of major interest in Table 11 is the relationship

Table 11. Average length of birth interval, by order of birth and number of children desired at first interview

Birth interval	Total	Desired family size at first interview				
		2	3	4	5	6+
		Average interval in months				
First	27	30	30	21	18	20
Second	37	47	38	29	23	19
Third	37	46	41	34	28	26
Fourth	34	35	35	37	29	25
Fifth	32	..	32	33	36	26
		Number of women				
First	814	240	256	248	32	26
Second	814	240	256	248	32	26
Third	555	95	174	220	31	25
Fourth	264	20	68	121	26	21
Fifth	116	4	22	51	16	18

31

between the number of children desired after the birth of the second child and the interval length of any given order. The greater the total number of children desired, the shorter is any given interval.[1] This generalization holds with the exception of the fourth or fifth birth intervals for women who at second parity did not want a child of the fourth or fifth order. For women who desired two or three children but had four or five, the higher order births are mostly unwanted births and consequently would not be expected to fall within the model of interval planning outlined above; that is, if they were unintended we should not expect their timing to derive from considerations of total family size and span of fertility. In general, these data are consistent with the notion that birth intervals are dependent upon the total family size desired. An alternative explanation might hold that reports of desired family size after the second birth are rationalized projections based on the rapidity of family building to date, and that the same physiological and sociological factors which resulted in the length of the first two intervals also conditioned subsequent intervals, independent of any "rational" element. While plausible, this alternative would require uncanny skill on the part of women to read so well the implication of their early fertility timing for completed family size (see Chapter IV); it becomes even less tenable in light of the evidence that *subsequent* contraceptive behavior is contingent upon the desired number expressed at the second birth (Chapter V).

The Span of Fertility

Birth intervals are combined in Table 12 to present data on the span of fertility by parity and number desired. Even though the average interval between births is nearly 3 years, women with six children have spent only 4 more years after marriage (and 5.5 more years after the first birth) in childbearing and associated role obligations than have women with two children. The marginal contribution

[1] See Westoff, Potter, and Sagi, *The Third Child*, pp. 56-65.

Table 12. Average interval between marriage and last birth and between first and last births, by parity and number of children desired at first interview

| Number of births | Total | Desired family size at first interview | | | |
		2	3	4	5+
		Marriage to last birth in years			
2	7.2	7.7	6.7	6.2	-
3	8.7	9.1	8.9	8.1	8.5
4	10.1	9.7	10.7	10.0	8.9
5	11.0	-	12.1	11.0	10.3
6	11.3	-	-	11.4	11.3
		First to last birth in years			
2	4.4	4.7	4.2	3.6	-
3	6.6	7.2	6.8	6.2	6.2
4	8.6	8.3	9.1	8.5	7.2
5	9.6	-	10.4	9.7	9.1
6	10.0	-	-	10.0	10.0
		Number of women			
2	259	145	82	28	2
3	291	74	106	99	10
4	148	17	46	68	13
5	77	2	17	40	18
6	27	2	4	10	10

to the overall span of fertility decreases with each increment in completed family size (first column of Table 12).

Again, it could be argued that poor contraceptive control leads both to short intervals and to larger families. However, it is of interest in Table 12 that among women who achieved the same parity, there is some evidence that parity was arrived at more quickly by women who originally desired more children than their final parity. In other words, it appears that the pace of family building is geared to desired family size so that the timing of fertility reflects that desired family size even when it is not achieved.

Some Correlates of Timing

As discussed above, the lengths of birth intervals of each order are correlated negatively with both the number of children desired and the number achieved. When the data for women of all parities are combined, age at marriage, education, and religion (coded Catholic–non-Catholic) are virtually uncorrelated with the lengths of birth intervals (first bank, Table 13). However, some interesting, though weak, correlations emerge when parity-specific comparisons are made; particularly noteworthy are the correlations with the overall span of fertility.

The relation between age at marriage and the span of fertility increases with the size of completed parity. This is not biologically necessary in the ranges involved here since "late" marriages are still at young enough ages that even five children could be born at longer than average intervals to most women. Among women with five children, the more rapid family building of those who married at later ages is probably a response to values about preferred upper age limits on childrearing.

Several types of pressures may operate to support such upper age limits. On the one hand, there is good reason for women to wish to confine the intensive demands of infant care to their younger years. At the same time, since most women have their children early there may be social sanctions against late childbearing; that is, women who are tied down by young children while their peers are not may experience difficulty "fitting into" the life styles and concerns of their peers.

At each parity, education is negatively related to the span of fertility. In part this relationship between education and

34

Table 13. Correlation between length of birth intervals and selected variables, by order of birth and current parity

	Birth interval					Marriage to last	First to last
	1st	2nd	3rd	4th	5th		
Total Sample							
Number of women	814	814	555	264	116	814	814
Number of births	-.32	-.34	-.41	-.38	-.37		
Desired family size	-.20	-.30	-.26	-.13	-.04		
Age at marriage	.07	-.03	-.06	-.05	-.09		
Education	.06	-.17	-.04	-.05	-.13		
Religion	.11	.05	.08	.00	.18		
Parity 2 (259)							
Desired family size	-.07	-.14				-.16	-.14
Age at marriage	.06	-.09				-.04	-.09
Education	.07	-.21				-.15	-.21
Religion	.01	-.06				-.04	-.06
Parity 3 (291)							
Desired family size	.04	-.11	-.10			-.11	-.15
Age at marriage	-.05	-.14	-.07			-.15	-.15
Education	.03	-.18	-.08			-.14	-.18
Religion	.04	-.12	-.07			.09	-.13
Parity 4 (148)							
Desired family size	.00	-.18	-.09	.04		-.12	-.13
Age at marriage	.09	-.06	-.18	-.03		-.10	-.15
Education	.12	-.19	-.08	-.08		-.14	-.21
Religion	-.05	-.01	.01	-.03		-.05	-.03
Parity 5 (77)							
Desired family size	-.13	-.36	-.25	.13	.04	-.21	-.19
Age at marriage	-.06	-.30	-.21	-.23	-.04	-.34	-.36
Education	.07	-.12	-.15	-.01	-.10	-.14	-.19
Religion	.07	.15	.23	-.24	.09	.08	.07

the spacing of births may result from the direct relationship between education and age at marriage. Since they marry later than less-educated women, those with greater education may build their families more quickly in order to achieve the number of children they desire while they are still in their preferred age range for child care. However, for women with only two children, education is related to the span of fertility while age at marriage is not. Perhaps for these women, the intervening variable is not desired age at childbearing so much as it is a desire to minimize the span of fertility in order to be freed for education-related female roles.

The results by religion are especially interesting. It is generally assumed that the Catholic orientation towards fertility involves shorter birth intervals as well as larger families. This, of course, is true from the perspective of all women who experience any given interval, though the differences are not great and are found primarily among college women.[2] However, the reason this is true is that Catholic women desire larger families, and consequently, at any given interval, proportionately more Catholic women are just "passing through" *en route* to a larger family size. When we compare the span of fertility for Catholics and non-Catholics by final parity we find that Catholics are as likely to have longer as shorter intervals than non-Catholics. All this is not really surprising, but it is relevant to the question of differences by religion in fertility control. The proposition is developed in Chapter V that Catholics do not differ from non-Catholics in their ability to control fertility after motivation as inferred from family-size desires is taken into account. These data on timing further support that contention.

It was suggested in the introduction of this chapter that spacing preferences are oriented more towards the desired duration of child care than towards specific lengths for given intervals. Table 14 illustrates how subsequent inter-

[2] Whelpton, Campbell and Patterson, *Fertility and Family Planning*, p. 324.

36

Table 14. Correlation between planning of births and length of birth intervals, by order of birth and parity

Length of birth interval	Planning of birth:				
	1	2	3	4	5
Parity 2 (259)					
Birth X	-.21	-.14			
Birth X + 1	.08				
Parity 3 (291)					
Birth X	-.26	-.20	-.03		
Birth X + 1	.07	.12			
Parity 4 (148)					
Birth X	-.19	-.39	-.24	-.14	
Birth X + 1	-.03	.04	.16		
Parity 5 (77)					
Birth X	-.28	-.35	-.07	-.20	-.14
Birth X + 1	-.09	-.06	.00	.00	

Note: Each birth was classified as "planned" (contraception inter-rupted in order to conceive, or not used for the explicit pur-pose of conceiving as soon as possible) or "unplanned" (con-traceptive failure, or non-use of contraception for other than spacing reasons). This variable, coded "0" if planned and "1" if unplanned, is correlated with the length (in months) of birth intervals. For example, in column 1 the planning status of the first birth is correlated with the length of the first birth interval in the first entry (-.21), and with the length of the second birth interval in the second entry (.08).

vals may compensate for previous interval lengths in the overall timing of fertility. Accidental pregnancy is nega-tively correlated with the length of the birth interval in which it occurs but uncorrelated or positively correlated with the length of the subsequent interval. In other words, women who experience a short birth interval because of

37

accidental pregnancy are likely to make up for that acceleration in timing by taking at least an average length of time to have the next child. Table 15 illustrates this compensat-

Table 15. Mean length of birth intervals for third parity women, by planning of births

Planning of births	Birth interval in months		Number of women
	Birth X	Birth X + 1	
Planned first			
Yes	29	32	161
No	19	35	129
Planned second			
Yes	37	43	167
No	28	49	123.
Planned third			
Yes	47		126
No	45		163

ing tendency in the average birth intervals of third parity women. While the compensation on the part of those experiencing an accidental birth is clear, the converse is not true. Women who plan interval X successfully and thus have a longer than average interval do not tend to experience shorter X + 1 intervals.

It is interesting to note that these relationships are observed in spite of the correlation between the planning statuses of successive intervals. The compensating tendency is sufficiently large to cancel out the shorter intervals contributed by women who failed in *both* intervals X and X + 1.

38

Unwanted Births and the Span of Fertility

The discussion to this point has been concerned with the response of the timing of births to the intended number of children and the desired duration of childbearing. A related question is the effect of unwanted births on the span of fertility. If women adjust the pace of their family building within limits of a desired duration of childbearing, then it is a significant sociological fact that unwanted births extend the period of childbearing beyond those limits for a substantial minority of women. Data from the 1965 National Fertility Study indicate that approximately 20 percent of recent births occurred to women who did not want to have another child.[3]

A Methodological Note

The analysis of birth interval data in cross-sectional samples is complicated by the fact that the interview truncates birth intervals for many women. This is much less a problem in our data than in most fertility surveys because the women in our sample are near the end of childbearing by the third interview. Nevertheless, 6 percent of the sample expect an additional birth and perhaps another 5 percent will have an unwanted birth in the remaining years of fecundity. While these additional births will not significantly affect the second and third birth intervals, expected additional births will constitute approximately 9 percent of all fourth births and 14 percent of all fifth births. These additional higher order births are likely to occur at longer intervals than comparable births to date and consequently represent a potential bias in the direction of the relationship between total parity and birth spacing. Under the assumption that on the average these additional births will occur 18 months after the date of the final interview, the difference in the span of fertility between parities two and

[3] Larry Bumpass and Charles F. Westoff, "The 'Perfect Contraceptive' Population," *Science* (Sept. 1970).

six is lengthened from 4.1 years to 5.3 years. Consequently although the data as reported here understate differences by final parity in the span of fertility, the bias does not appear large enough to be responsible for the patterns observed.

IV · The Prediction of Fertility

The relationship between family-size desires and subsequent fertility has received considerable attention both because of its relevance for the projection of fertility and because of its intrinsic sociological interest.[1]

Many couples have more or fewer children than they initially wanted, because of contraceptive failure, infecundity, or changes in the number wanted. Family-size desires are not fixed over the course of marriage but vary with social and economic contingencies as well as in response to actual fertility.[2] As reported in Chapter II, family-size desires were stable over the 8-year study period for only one-third of the respondents. Much of this apparent change may result from unreliability, particularly in measurement techniques, rather than instability of the number wanted. Even so, the relationship between desired and actual fertility will depend upon the point at which the desires are measured, and the time at which the second child is born may be the most relevant for this question. Since virtually all women want at least two children, reports of desired family size prior to the achievement of this minimum may be selected more randomly from the range of "acceptable" family sizes. Indeed, the number of children wanted by women shortly before marriage is not strongly related to the number they eventually achieve.[3] Beyond second parity, reports of family-size desires may increasingly include rationalizations of unwanted births. Here we shall focus on the extent to which family-size desires expressed after the birth of the second child are

[1] See Ryder and Westoff, "The Trend of Expected Parity"; and Jacob S. Siegel and Donald S. Akers, "Some Aspects of the Use of Birth Expectations Data from Sample Surveys for Population Projections," *Demography* 6, No. 2 (1969): 101-16, for current discussion of this issue.

[2] Freedman, Coombs, and Bumpass, "Stability and Change."

[3] Charles F. Westoff, Elliot G. Mishler, and E. Lowell Kelly, "Preferences in Size of Family and Eventual Fertility Twenty Years After," *American Journal of Sociology* 62 (1957): 491-97.

realized in completed fertility, and on subgroup variation in this realization.

Estimated Completed Fertility

At the time of the third interview the women in our sample are, on the average, 36 years of age and have an average interval of 5.5 years since the birth of their last child. While most of these women have completed their families, 8 percent indicate that they "definitely or probably" expect more children. Those expecting more children are generally younger and have relatively short open intervals—one third are currently pregnant. On the other hand, women not expecting more children are generally older, and have relatively long intervals since the birth of their last child. Estimated completed family size is based almost wholly on the respondents' stated expectations.[4] By the third interview 98 percent of all children expected have been born. While we know that there will be a few subsequent pregnancies to women who think that their families are completed, we have not attempted to predict which women will have these pregnancies. But even if allowance is made for accidental fertility over the fertile years remaining, children born by the third interview probably still represent over 90 percent of the children that will ultimately be borne by these women.

Desired Family Size

The wives were asked at the first interview how many children they wanted altogether, counting the two they had at the time. They were then asked how sure they felt about this number and whether they might want more or fewer children. These two measures were combined to

[4] In only ten cases was a completed family size assigned that differed from the respondent's expectations. Illustrative of these is a 37-year-old woman who expects two more births but who had trouble with her last two pregnancies, reports she is in menopause, and who in the absence of contraception has not had a pregnancy in the last 8 years. This case was assigned a completed family size equal to current parity.

42

form an index of the wife's total family-size desires. For example, a woman who replied that she wanted three children altogether "but might want more" was scaled higher on the index than a woman who wanted three children and was certain, but lower than a woman who wanted four children and was certain. In the construction of this index approximately one-fourth of the cases were scaled upward or downward on the basis of certainty. It is interesting that for correlational purposes this procedure offers no improvement over the respondent's desires taken at face value: the two measures correlate exactly the same (.56) with estimated completed fertility. While couples who said they might want more or fewer children than their stated desires vary consistently in completed fertility from couples who were certain of the number they wanted, this kind of detail cannot be maintained for comparisons within categories of family-size desires. Consequently, the respondent's stated family-size desires are employed here without regard to the degree of certainty.

Aggregate Prediction

The average number of children wanted by women after the birth of their second child predicts very well the average size of their completed families (Table 16). The average family size desired at the first interview and average estimated completed family size some 8 years later are identical for the total sample, and vary hardly at all within religious or educational subgroups. Active Protestants, Jewish women, and women who have attended college (those most inclined to early contraception) have slightly fewer children than originally wanted. Completed family size is slightly greater than originally desired among Other Protestants, and the two measures are identical among both Active and Other Catholics (although this results from a large number of compensating discrepancies).

The patterns by family-planning success are as we would expect. Women who plan most of their pregnancies have slightly fewer children than they originally wanted. Earlier

43

Table 16. Mean number of children desired at first interview, by selected
characteristics; and mean completed parity, by number of
children desired at first interview and selected characteristics

Characteristic	Mean number of children desired	Mean completed parity					
			Number of children desired at first interview				
		Total	2	3	4	5	6+
Total	3.3	3.3	2.5	3.0	3.7	4.8	5.6
Religion							
Protestants	3.0	3.0	2.6	3.0	3.6	...	...
Active	3.1	3.0	2.4	2.9	3.6	...	...
Other	2.9	3.0	2.7	3.0	3.6	...	...
Catholics	3.6	3.6	2.5	3.3	3.9	4.8	5.6
Active	4.3	4.3	...	3.5	4.1	4.9	6.0
Other	3.4	3.4	2.5	3.3	3.8	...	...
Jews	2.7	2.6	2.2	2.6	3.5	...	...
Education							
0-11 years	3.1	3.3	2.6	3.2	3.7	...	...
12 years	3.2	3.3	2.5	3.1	3.7	4.9	5.5
College	3.4	3.2	2.4	2.8	3.8	...	5.8
Proportion of pregnancies that were planned:							
All or majority	3.1	2.9	2.3	2.9	3.4	...	...
Half or fewer	3.4	3.6	2.7	3.2	4.0	5.0	5.6

... Fewer than 10 sample cases

studies have indicated that success in controlling fertility
may lead to the achievement of smaller families than initially desired.[5] The longer a couple delays the occurrence
of a "wanted" birth, the more opportunity the wife has to

[5] Westoff, Mishler, and Kelly, "Preferences in Size of Family and
Eventual Fertility Twenty Years After," p. 494; Freedman, Coombs,
and Bumpass, "Stability and Change," p. 267.

acquire role patterns not defined in terms of early child-care responsibility. At some point that next birth may no longer be as desirable. In addition, the delay of a wanted birth increases the possibility that subfecundity will prevent that birth. On the other hand, inability to control the spacing of a desired birth, particularly if it is the last birth wanted, may well indicate inability to prevent an unwanted birth. Given the prevalence of unwanted fertility among American women,[6] it seems likely that women who have planned half or fewer of their births may exceed their desired family size by more than the 0.2 indicated in Table 16, since a large portion of the future unwanted births in this sample may occur to these women.

Average completed family size increases consistently with each increment in the family size wanted at the first interview. However, the agreement between average desired and average completed fertility results from compensating tendencies to have more or fewer children than originally wanted, depending upon the original number wanted. Women who after the birth of their second child said they desired no more children had a total of 2.5 children, whereas women who wanted six or more children had only 5.6 children on the average.

The fact that women who desired no more children had an additional 0.5 births per woman might be interpreted as indicating either a high instability of family-size desires or a poor record of contraceptive efficacy. Neither seems to be the case. Of the women who originally wanted only two children but who have borne three or more children, four-fifths report their last pregnancy as unplanned. Apparently most of the excess over the number originally desired is a result of contraceptive failure. This, however, does not reflect a low level of contraceptive efficacy. Women who want only two children achieve their desired number very early in the childbearing years, and consequently face longer exposure to the risk of unwanted births than do women desiring larger families. One-third of these women

[6] Bumpass and Westoff, "The 'Perfect Contraceptive' Population."

experienced at least one accidental pregnancy, but this is consistent with a reasonably high contraceptive efficacy of over .995 per fertile period over the average of 7 years since the birth of their second child.

On the other hand, women who initially wanted six or more children could reevaluate these high family-size desires in light of the experience of subsequent births, with less exposure to the risk of unwanted births. Many of these women apparently revised their desired family size downward.

A direct relationship between the number of children desired at the first interview and completed fertility can be observed within each of the categories of religion, education, and family-planning success in Tables 16 and 17. It is

Table 17. Mean number of children desired at first interview, by religion and education; and mean completed parity, by number of children desired at first interview, religion, and education

Religion and education	Mean number of children desired	Mean completed parity					
			Number of children desired at first interview				
		Total	2	3	4	5	6+
Protestants							
0-11 years	3.1	3.4	2.6	3.3	4.0	...	...
12 years	2.9	2.9	2.6	2.9	3.5	...	...
College	3.0	2.9	2.6	2.9	3.4	...	...
Catholics							
0-11 years	3.2	3.2	2.6	3.1	3.6	...	...
12 years	3.7	3.7	2.5	3.4	3.8	5.0	5.5
College	4.1	4.1	...	3.1	4.3	...	5.9
Jews							
0-11 years	...	...	...	...	...	...	...
12 years	2.4	2.3	2.1	2.5	...	...	...
College	3.1	2.7	2.2	2.6	3.4	...	...

... Fewer than 10 sample cases

46

of additional interest that among women who wanted the same number of children at the first interview (reading down the columns) there are still differences in completed fertility by religion, education, and family-planning success. However our concern here is with the relation between desired and actual fertility for these subgroups; the question of socioeconomic differentials in fertility and their interaction with religion and age at marriage is taken up in Chapter VI.

When we consider religion and education simultaneously (Table 17), the only subgroups for which there are marked differences between the average number of children desired at first interview and average fertility are low-education Protestant women and high-education Jewish women. The fact that the latter achieve substantially fewer children than initially desired may well be attributable to the effects of fertility control discussed above, as this is the subgroup with the highest level of success at fertility control. The fact that low-education Protestant women exceed their initial desires more than low-education Catholic women may result in part from earlier age at marriage for this group and hence longer exposure to the risk of unwanted fertility.

Patterns of Discrepancies

We have observed that the average number of children desired after the birth of the second child predicts closely the average size of completed families. Nevertheless, only 41 percent of these women achieved exactly the number of children they reported wanting at the first interview, while 14 percent had two children more or fewer than originally wanted (Table 18).

The relationship between original preferences and completed fertility varies systematically with religion, education, and family-planning success. The proportion of women who exactly achieved their desired family size is highest for Jewish women (55 percent) and lowest for Catholic women (35 percent), is directly related to edu-

47

Table 18. Comparison between number of children desired at first interview and completed fertility, by selected characteristics

Charac- teristics	Fertility exceeds desires by		Fertility same as desired	Fertility is less than desires by		Total	
	2+	1		1	2+	Percent	Number
Total	8	22	41	24	6	100	814
Religion							
Protestants	8	22	44	23	3	100	333
Active	4	24	43	25	4	100	136
Other	11	21	44	22	2	100	197
Catholics	9	24	35	23	9	100	383
Active	13	18	35	20	15	100	95
Other	8	26	35	24	7	100	288
Jews	4	10	55	29	2	100	98
Education							
0-11 years	8	30	37	21	5	100	153
12 years	9	22	41	21	7	100	428
College	7	15	43	31	4	100	233
Proportion of pregnancies that were planned:							
All or majority	4	16	48	27	5	100	380
Half or fewer	12	27	34	21	6	100	434

cation, and, as expected, is considerably higher for women
who planned all or most of their pregnancies than for
women who planned half or fewer of their pregnancies.

The size and direction of discrepancies is also related to
these characteristics. Over one-fourth of the Active Catholics have a completed family size that differs from their
original desires by two or more children. However, these

women were as likely to have fewer as they were to have more children than originally wanted, with the net result that the average completed family size is the same as the average family size desired. These discrepancies of two or more children between desired and achieved family size occur for women for whom average desired family size was either relatively high or relatively low compared to the average for all Catholics. Among women desiring very large families, further experience with childrearing may well lead to a more realistic family size goal. Among those desiring relatively small families, we could be observing the normative influence of Catholic reference groups upon women who are active in that community. However, the fact that Other Protestants are almost as likely as Active Catholics to exceed their original desires by two or more children makes it more likely that these are simply women who were unable to prevent unwanted births—four-fifths report their last pregnancy as unplanned.

Though it has been argued that fertility control prior to the achievement of desired family size is not highly predictive of the ability to prevent unwanted births, there is a relationship between the proportion of pregnancies that were planned and the achievement of desired family size. This is not surprising of course since the measure used relates to all pregnancies, with the consequence that some of the unplanned pregnancies are also unwanted pregnancies. Women who planned the majority of their pregnancies were more likely to achieve their desired family size than women who planned fewer; and much of the difference is a result of fertility in excess of desires among the poorer planners.

Perhaps as a consequence of the above relationship, sub-groups which are most likely to use early and effective contraception are most likely to achieve their desires exactly, and to have fewer children than originally wanted if they fail to achieve their initial preferences. By religion, Jewish women are most likely to achieve their desires exactly or, if they fail, to have fewer children than wanted. By edu-

49

cation, women who did not complete high school are most likely to exceed the family size they initially wanted.

Family-Size Desires at Second Interview

Respondents were again asked about their desired family size at the second interview. While theoretical interest centers on the first-interview reports (because of the longer interval of time involved and because later reports include excess fertility), the convergence of the number desired and the number achieved over the process of childbearing is important whatever the nature of that convergence. While family-size desires at the first interview are correlated .56 with completed fertility, the correlation is .67 between the second interview desires and completed fertility.

We expect women to become more certain of the number of children they want as they near the end of family building in the same sense that accuracy increases as the distance to the target decreases, but it is also true that the numbers reported as "desired" increasingly include unwanted births. It is impossible to unravel completely the causal ordering of changes in fertility desires and actual fertility. However it is evident that insofar as fertility behavior responds to changes in desires, the lead time is short. Changes in fertility preferences between the first and second interviews (a 3-year interval), while correlated .25 with fertility in that interval, are unrelated to subsequent fertility.

Other Variables Associated with Completed Fertility

In addition to the wife's desired family size there are a number of other variables measured at the first interview which are correlated with completed fertility. Among these are: the husband's desired family size, fertility-planning success by the first interview, and the interval between marriage and the birth of the second child. These are all correlated with completed fertility, but they are also correlated with one another (Table 19). Rather than attempt-

Table 19. Correlations among fertility variables: 814 women

	F	W	H	P	I
F	-				
W	.56	-			
H	.49	.64	-		
P	.31	.21	.20	-	
I	-.47	-.36	-.31	-.36	-

Item identification: F - estimated completed family size

                                   W - wife's family-size desires at first interview

                                   H - husband's family-size desires at first interview

                                   P - family-planning success by first interview

                                   I - interval between marriage and birth of second child

ing to partial out the net effect of each on completed fertility,[7] we consider the three following questions concerning the increment each provides for our prediction of completed fertility:

1) While we often focus attention on the number of children desired by the wife, do the husband's family-size de-

[7] For discussion of the problems involved in the attempt to partial out the net effects of highly correlated variables, see Robert A. Gordon, "Issues in Multiple Regression," *American Journal of Sociology* 73, No. 5 (1968): 592-616.

sires provide additional relevant information about completed fertility?

2) Fertility-planning success before the birth of the second child is related to the size of completed families. While this relationship may result from a tendency to have unwanted births among women who do not plan their first two births, it may simply reflect an early casual attitude toward contraception among couples who desire larger families. Does family-planning success by the second birth tell us anything about completed fertility that we do not know from family-size preferences?

3) The interval between marriage and the second birth is negatively correlated with the size of completed families. This interval reflects the combined influence of contraceptive failures, fecundity problems, and preferences about birth intervals. Undoubtedly, all these factors are to some extent taken into account in the desired family size husbands and wives report. But does the interval between marriage and the second birth contribute additional explained variance in completed fertility over the variance explained by family-size desires and fertility-planning success?

With completed family size as the dependent variable, the coefficients of determination (R^2) for the wife's desires, and for combinations of other variables with the wife's desires, are presented in Table 20. The husband's family-size desires add somewhat to our ability to predict completed fertility, while the planning of the first two births adds virtually nothing. However, our prediction is improved markedly when we include the interval between marriage and the second birth. Clearly, the length of the first two intervals is associated with the limiting effects of both age and fecundity unforeseen by the couple formulating their family-size desires. But, in addition, the time taken to reach second parity may indicate effects on fertility of the interests and activities of the parents which were not reflected in first-interview desires but which had a continued influence on fertility.

Table 20. The multiple prediction of estimated completed family size, by religion and education

Religion and education	W	W & H	Coefficient of determination for: W, H, & P	W, H, & I	Number of cases
Total	.31	.34	.35	.42	814
Religion					
Protestants	.18	.22	.26	.32	333
Active	.27	.30	.33	.45	136
Other	.14	.18	.18	.25	197
Catholics	.29	.31	.34	.39	383
Active	.28	.28	.28	.38	95
Other	.24	.28	.29	.35	288
Jews	.31	.34	.36	.39	98
Education					
0-11 years	.27	.32	.33	.40	153
12 years	.29	.31	.32	.40	428
College	.39	.44	.44	.48	233

Item identification: W – wife's family-size desires at first interview
H – husband's family-size desires at first interview
P – family-planning success by first interview
I – interval between marriage and birth of second child

Summary and Conclusions

In conclusion, these longitudinal data support the thesis that family-size desires at second parity constitute goals for subsequent fertility behavior. In fact, at the aggregate level for the religious and educational subgroups considered here, average completed family size is *very* close to the average number of children desired at the first interview (although there are important subgroup variations in the manner in which this is achieved).

Nevertheless, the majority of women do not finish with exactly the number wanted after their second child was born. One-third of the variance in the completed fertility of couples is "explained" by the wife's family-size desires; the proportion of explained variance increases to two-fifths when we include the husband's first interview desires and the interval between marriage and second birth. We have suggested that the achievement of second parity is the point at which expressed family-size desires are most representative of the goals which will regulate the fertility process over the remainder of the fertile years, and yet most of the variance in completed family size is unexplained by desires at second parity. Given the complexity of the life cycle it would be naive to expect otherwise. The level of the correlation is attenuated not only by contraceptive failure and fecundity but also by the instability and unreliability of initial desires. Nevertheless, family-size desires are clearly a relevant variable in the determination of fertility. The analysis of contraceptive efficacy reported in the next chapter further documents the fact that these desires are goals regulating subsequent behavior, and that, as targets toward which couples are aiming, these desires are important for the study of fertility even though the targets may often be missed.

V · The Improvement of Contraceptive Use

We have seen in earlier chapters that both the timing of births and size of completed families vary systematically with the number of children desired after the birth of the second child. In this chapter we will explore the changes in contraceptive use that occur as women approach and achieve the number of children they wanted 8 years earlier.

Women in the United States typically marry at young ages, space their children relatively close together, and achieve their desired family size while they are still young. As a consequence, they face a long period of exposure to the risk of unwanted pregnancies. If even a moderate proportion are to survive this risk period without experiencing an unwanted pregnancy, contraceptive practices must change radically as women achieve their desired family size. If contraception were practiced during a 10-year risk period with the efficacy observed among couples using contraception prior to the first pregnancy, two-thirds of the couples would experience at least one unwanted pregnancy, two-fifths would have three or more unwanted pregnancies.[1] Nevertheless, white women 35-39 in the United States in 1955, 1960, and 1965 claimed to have avoided excess fertility in over 75 percent of the cases.[2] If such reports are valid, there must be marked improvement in contraceptive efficacy as a cohort ages.

Analysis of data from the first two interviews revealed that the closer a pregnancy interval is to a woman's desired family size, the greater the efficacy of contraceptive use during that interval.[3] It is now possible to observe this pattern for women who are near the end of their childbearing years and to exploit the longitudinal study

[1] Westoff, Potter and Sagi, *The Third Child*, p. 46.
[2] Freedman, Whelpton, and Campbell, *Family Planning*, p. 83; Whelpton, Campbell, and Patterson, *Fertility and Family Planning*, p. 245; Ryder and Westoff, *Reproduction in the United States: 1965*, Chapter 9, Table 6.
[3] Westoff, Potter, and Sagi, *The Third Child*, pp. 38-44.

design to test the relation between desires expressed after the birth of the second child and subsequent behavior.

Changes in the Use of Contraception

The probability of conception declines over the later childbearing years, independent of the use of contraception, as a result of declining fecundity and decreasing coital frequency; but it is clear from a comparison with the fertility levels of noncontracepting populations that these factors contribute little to the degree of fertility control experienced by American women. The major part of increased fertility control appears to result from increased proportions using contraception, from shifts among women using contraception to more effective methods, and from more faithful use of whatever methods are being employed.

There is a very strong relation between the number of children desired and the use of contraception during the first two birth intervals. This relationship diminishes in the later birth intervals (Table 21) because even for couples who want large families there is considerable pressure to use contraception after a while in order to ease the pace of family building experienced while not using contraception. Indeed, we saw in Chapter III that short birth intervals tend to be compensated for by longer subsequent intervals.

Table 22 traces the progress of the women in our sample through the childbearing years by presenting their distribution by method of contraception used before the first, second, and last birth, and by method used at the time of the third interview. In order to simplify the discussion of changes in the methods of contraception used, contraceptive methods have been grouped into four major categories: "Effective" methods include the pill, diaphragm and jelly, condom, withdrawal, or combinations or alterations among these; "Rhythm only" is distinguished from "Rhythm combinations"; and the "Other" category is a residual category including primarily jelly, douche, or alterations between

Table 21. Percent using contraception, by birth interval and number of children desired at first interview

Desired family size at first interview	Birth interval				
	1st	2nd	3rd	4th	5th
	Percent reporting use of contraception in interval				
2	72	89	88	90	..
3	57	83	89	93	91
4	45	79	84	87	90
5	22	53	81	85	81
6 +	8	35	68	67	72
	Number of couples				
2	240	240	95	20	4
3	256	256	174	68	22
4	248	248	220	121	51
5	32	32	31	26	16
6 +	26	26	25	21	18

these and other methods. Women who did not use contraception during any interval were asked their reasons for non-use and we have classified these reasons as either "rational" or "nonrational." Non-use of contraception was considered rational only for women who gave as their sole reason either that they wanted a child as soon as possible or that they feared difficulty in conceiving. All other reasons for not using contraception were considered to be nonrational from a family-planning perspective. Women who reported that they had never used contraception are classified separately, since we have only their reasons for current non-use.

The increase in contraceptive use over the course of mar-

Table 22. Distribution by use or non-use of contraception and method used, and interval of use and religion

Religion and interval	Total	Sterile	Users					Non-users			
			Total	Effective	Other	Rhythm	Rhythm Comb.	Total	Nonrational	Rational	Never
Total (814)											
First birth	100		54	34	6	8	6	46	15	22	9
Second birth	100		80	49	6	16	9	20	4	7	9
Last birth	100		86	50	5	20	11	14	2	6	6
Current	100	11	80	50	6	13	10	9	1	5	3
Protestant (333)											
First birth	100		63	42	8	4	9	37	13	21	3
Second birth	100		86	61	8	6	11	14	2	9	3
Last birth	100		87	62	6	5	14	13	2	8	3
Current	100	15	78	57	7	4	10	7	1	6	-
Catholic (383)											
First birth	100		39	18	4	12	5	61	21	25	15
Second birth	100		83	29	6	30	8	27	6	6	15
Last birth	100		82	30	4	38	10	18	2	6	10
Current	100	6	81	41	7	23	10	13	2	5	6
Active Catholic (95)											
First birth	100		27	5	2	19	1	73	13	31	29
Second birth	100		49	7	1	39	1	51	12	10	29
Last birth	100		80	9	1	67	3	20	3	2	15
Current	100	5	74	17	6	39	12	21	3	6	12
Jewish (98)											
First birth	100		83	76	3	-	4	17	3	14	-
Second birth	100		93	89	1	1	2	7	2	5	-
Last birth	100		94	87	2	2	3	6	2	4	-
Current	100	14	83	73	3	1	6	3	-	1	2

riage is readily apparent in Table 22. At any point in time, some women will not be using contraception either because they want to conceive as soon as possible or, as is the case at the third interview, because they are currently pregnant. By the third interview, 96 percent of the women were either using contraception, sterile, pregnant, or trying to become pregnant.

While there are strong differences by religion in the use of contraception, a marked increase in its use over the course of marriage is observed within each broad religious grouping. Non-use is highest among Active Catholics, but even here the proportion reporting non-use declines from 73 percent before the first birth to 21 percent by the third interview. By the third interview, 85 percent of the Active Catholics are either using contraception, sterile, pregnant, or trying to become pregnant. Although many women do not use contraception early in marriage, as desired family size is achieved all but a small minority adopt contraception in the attempt to prevent having more children than they want.

With respect to the types of methods used, as couples near the end of childbearing increased protection against unwanted births results, in the aggregate, not from a net shift to the more effective methods but from sterilization on the part of many couples. As many women were using effective methods before their second child as were using these methods at the time of the third interview (Table 22). (Active Catholics are an exception to this, with the proportion using effective methods increasing from 9 percent before their last birth to 17 percent by the third interview. Also worth noting is the shift among Active Catholics after the last birth from rhythm only to rhythm used in combination with other methods.) Eleven percent of the couples are sterile at the third interview, most of these presumably for contraceptive reasons. When asked what, if anything, they did after the birth of their last child in order "to make sure that you wouldn't become pregnant again," 38 cases indicate sterilization of the wife,

39 couples sterilization of the husband.[4] While these couples have opted for the most effective "method" of contraception, they are not included in our analysis of contraceptive efficacy since they face no "risk"; and since they are not included, any changes in methods of use relevant to increased efficacy will have to occur among the other methods.

When we consider the distribution of users of contraception by method and interval of use (Table 23), it is clear that increases in efficacy do not result from a net shift to more effective methods. In fact, when we compare

Table 23.· Distribution of women using contraception, by method used and interval of use

Interval	Method					Number of women
	Effective	Other	Rhythm	Rhythm comb.	Total	
First birth	64	10	14	12	100	440
Second birth	61	8	20	11	100	655
Last birth	58	5	24	13	100	696
Current	64	8	16	12	100	650

[4] The sterile category thus includes 12 cases for whom the contraceptive intent of sterilization is ambiguous, although the contraceptive consequences are the same. The extent of sterilization is underestimated in these data since 13 cases known to be sterile at the time of the first interview were not reinterviewed.

all women who used contraception before their first birth to all women who used contraception before their last birth, there is a net decrease in the proportion using effective methods. This occurs because of the inflows of women who had previously not used contraception but who began use with the less effective methods. By the third interview, the proportion using effective methods is the same as the proportion using these methods before the first interview.

In the aggregate there is no increase over the course of marriage in the proportion of users who employ effective methods. However the question of whether individual women are more likely to use effective methods of contraception as they grow older still remains. Table 24 indicates

Table 24. Method of contraception used before second birth, by method used at time of third interview, for women not pregnant or trying to become pregnant at time of third interview

Method before birth of second child	Current method				Total	Number of women
	Effective	Sterile	Other	Non-use		
Effective	65	13	20	2	100	394
Other	41	9	48	3	100	231
Non-use	37	12	36	15	100	150
Total	52	11	32	6	100	775

that while some women shift from effective to other methods, there is a higher probability that former users of other methods will either be using effective methods or be sterilized by the third interview. One-fifth of those using effective methods before their second child are using other methods by the third interview, whereas half of the women who did not use effective methods before their second birth were either sterile or using effective methods by the third interview. (The fact that these individual patterns do not

61

result in a net aggregate shift toward effective methods is a product of the different sized numerical bases involved.) Sterilization is an important part of the contraceptive protection of women near the end of childbearing. Any increase in efficacy we observe for the contracepting population does not tell the whole story, since 11 percent of the women have chosen a completely effective method not included in our analysis of failure rates.

Changes among "Users" in the Efficacy of Use

The measure of contraceptive efficacy employed is the "cumulative failure rate," the proportion of couples who could be expected to fail in contraception over a 1-year period of exposure.[5] This measure is calculated by life-table procedures and consequently takes into account the differing monthly probabilities of conception and the fact that some users have intentionally discontinued contraception. Months of contraceptive exposure for any given birth interval were calculated by subtracting from that birth interval 9 months for pregnancy time, and 2 months for postpartum amenorrhea. The "open interval" is included in the calculations for birth orders one greater than parity. Adjustments were made for separations of over 3 months duration that occurred during the first 12 months of contraceptive exposure in any interval. In addition, because of the extreme unreliability involved in reporting dates of miscarriages, we excluded from the analysis of any given birth interval couples who reported a fetal death in that interval. The result of this exclusion of fetal deaths may be that we somewhat overestimate the prevention of unwanted conceptions, but underestimate the prevention of unwanted births. This analysis focuses exclusively on pregnancies terminating in live birth not only because of the unreliability of miscarriage data but primarily because we are concerned with the relation between desired family size

[5] Robert G. Potter, "Application of Life Table Techniques to Measurement of Contraceptive Effectiveness," *Demography* 3, No. 2 (1966): 297-304.

and the family-building process. If pregnancy order were employed instead, the analysis would be muddied by the fact that for some women pregnancies of an order higher than desired family size are necessary in order to achieve that desired size.

We have seen that among women using contraception, the proportion using the more effective methods does not increase over the later childbearing years. To what extent are methods used with greater effectiveness after desired family size has been achieved? A cumulative failure rate of .32 is estimated for women who used contraception before their first birth; and a rate of .25, for women who used contraception between their first and second birth (Table 25). Failure rates of this magnitude imply that virtually all women would experience an accidental pregnancy over a 10-year risk period if there were no improvement of contraception. For birth intervals after the second, women are divided on the basis of the number of children desired at the first interview into those who seek to *prevent* a birth of a higher order and those who use contraception to *delay* a birth of this order. For example, women who said at the first interview that they desired only two children are assumed to be attempting to prevent a third birth, whereas women who wanted three or more children are considered to be seeking to control only the timing of this birth.

Although family-size desires change over time, the predictive value of these desires for future contraceptive performance is impressive. Women who, on the basis of family-size desires at first interview, were seeking to prevent a birth of the third or fourth order experienced failure rates in these intervals substantially lower than the failure rates experienced by contraceptors in the first two intervals; their failure rates are also lower than the failure rates experienced by women who were "delaying" births of the third or fourth order. Cumulative failure rates of .06 and .08 are calculated for "preventers" at the third and fourth birth intervals respectively, as compared with rates of .23 and .17 respectively for "delayers" in these intervals. Pre-

63

Table 25. Cumulative failure rates by interval of contraceptive use, reason for use (P = preventing; D = delaying), religion, and education

Religion and education	First	Second	Third P	Third D	Fourth P	Fourth D	Fifth P	Fifth D
			Cumulative failure rate					
Total	.32	.25	.06	.23	.08	.17	.14	.35
Religion								
Protestant	.36	.29	.06	.18	.06	.16	.11	...
Catholic	.34	.27	.05	.29	.09	.19	.17	.36
Jewish	.19	.09	.03	.11	.11	...	...	...
Education								
Less than 12 years	.37	.30	.05	.17	.14	.31	.15	...
12 years	.32	.25	.06	.27	.07	.18	.14	...
College	.30	.25	.02	.19	.05	.07	.08	...
			Number of couples					
Total	396	596	201	427	221	214	171	33
Religion								
Protestant	187	266	109	160	100	64	64	1
Catholic	134	247	58	222	94	137	99	31
Jewish	75	83	34	45	21	13	8	1
Education								
Less than 12 years	63	113	38	75	47	33	42	3
12 years	197	304	114	220	111	121	93	17
College	136	180	49	132	57	71	36	13

venters in the fifth interval do not fare as well, although they experience much lower failure rates than delayers in this interval. One reason for the higher failure rate for preventers in the fifth birth interval is the accumulation of women who were preventers at earlier intervals, but who also failed there.

Although there are substantial differences between Catholics and non-Catholics in the methods of contraception used, there is little difference between the two groups in efficacy of fertility control after motivation to control fertility as inferred from the number of children desired is taken into account. The cumulative failure rates for preventers are virtually identical; and while the rates for delayers are somewhat higher for Catholics, this undoubtedly reflects the fact that Catholic delayers in the third interval are further from their ultimate family-size goal than are non-Catholic delayers. When compared to the other religious groups, Jewish women were much more successful at controlling their fertility when they were spacing births, and somewhat more successful when preventing.

Since the proportion of contraceptors using effective methods does not increase over the course of marriage, the observed increase in contraceptive efficacy must result from more successful use of whatever methods are employed. It does not necessarily follow that this increase in effectiveness is the same for all types of methods. However the data in Table 26 suggest that motivation to control fertility as implied by desired family size affects the success with which both rhythm and the effective methods are employed. Among women using effective methods before their second birth, the cumulative failure rate was .09 for women who desired two children at the first interview, as opposed to a rate of .23 for women who desired three or more children. While the failure rates for women using the rhythm method are considerably higher, those desiring two children had a lower failure rate (.28) than those desiring three or more (.38). Among women who used effective

65

Table 26. Cumulative failure rates, by type of method and desires for two or more than two children at the first interview

Interval and number of children desired	Method used in second interval		Method used in first and second intervals	
	Effective	Rhythm	Effective	Rhythm
	Cumulative failure rate			
First interval				
2	-	-	.22	...
3+	-	-	.22	.45
Second interval				
2	.09	.28	.06	...
3+	.23	.38	.17	.33
	Number of couples			
First interval				
2	-	-	99	5
3+	-	-	125	33
Second interval				
2	149	18	99	5
3+	220	99	125	33

methods in both the first and second intervals, the effect of desired family size on effectiveness of contraception increases as that family size is approached. While there is little difference in contraceptive effectiveness during the first interval between women desiring two children and those desiring more, there is a considerable difference in the second interval failure rates.

The contraceptive effectiveness among preventers represents a marked improvement in efficacy over that observed early in marriage, but are the failure rates of preventers compatible with the degree of fertility control claimed by older women in the national fertility surveys? In answering this question we have to take into account the fact that because of sterilization many couples are not exposed to the risk of conception, and that it is likely that the decline of fecundity and coital frequency as well as increased experience with contraceptives reduce the risk of unintended conception.

The third interval failure rate for women who were 30 years of age or older at the first interview and who said they wanted only two children (preventers) is .03 compared with the rate of .07 observed for all third interval preventers. If we assume that .07 represents an upper limit and .03 a lower limit and that risk declines evenly over the 10-year period, and if we take into account sterilizations, 64 percent of our sample would be expected to be successful in preventing an unwanted conception. If the women 35-39 in the national fertility studies experienced a failure rate of .03 over an average 4 years of remaining risk, the proportion preventing an unwanted conception would be around 65 percent. While the comparison is necessarily crude and does not take into account induced abortions, it is apparent that the claims of women 35-39 in the national fertility studies are not inconsistent with the levels of contraceptive efficacy observed among women seeking to prevent an unwanted birth.

Sources of Improved Contraception

We have observed both that the efficacy of contraceptive use increases over the course of marriage and that users, on the average, do not shift to the more effective methods. Consequently whatever methods are employed are used with greater efficacy as women achieve the number of children they desire to have. This improved efficacy may result from the combination of higher motivation and increased contraceptive experience with declining fecundity and coital frequency. While reports of "chance taking" with contraceptives are highly unreliable, some estimate of the effect of increased motivation may be indicated (Table 27) by the decline in the proportion who say they occasionally skip use of contraception from 31 percent at

Table 27.. "Chance-taking" as reported at the second and third interviews, by type of method used

Report	Total	Method	
		Effective	Other
		Percent who take chances	
Second interview	31	30	34
Third interview	21	16	28
		Percent who say they take chances outside of the "safe" period	
Third interview	6	5	7

the second interview to 21 percent by the third interview. By the third interview only 6 percent say they take chances outside of the "safe period."

Declining fecundity is virtually impossible to measure independently of measures of conception. However, if we compare the average ages of preventers and delayers at the third birth interval, we find that those who desired only two children (preventers) were 29.2 years of age on the average compared with an average age of 26.5 for women wanting three or more children. Only a 3 percent difference in the number of fecund women per thousand married women would be expected between women of these average ages.[6] Consequently, it is unlikely that fecundity differences implied by the age difference contribute to the marked differences in contraceptive efficiency observed between preventers and delayers.

The decline of coital frequency with age decreases exposure to the risk of unwanted pregnancy. In fact, part of the decline associated with age may reflect increased anxiety about accidental pregnancy after the number of children desired has been achieved. If this were the case, we might expect coital frequency to decline with age more rapidly for couples using the less effective methods, since the anxiety about an unwanted conception should be the greatest for such couples. Indeed, coital frequency declined much more rapidly between the second and third interviews for non-sterile couples who were not using effective methods at the third interview than for couples using effective methods, even though the second interview rates and the mean ages of the women were identical (Table 28). While the 18 percent decline in coital frequency among women not using effective methods may contribute somewhat to their ability to avoid unwanted pregnancies, it is unlikely that a decline of 5 percent among women using effective methods contributes much at all to the sharp increase in efficacy observed among such women after they

[6] Louis Henry, *Fécondité des Mariages* (Presses Universitaires de France, 1953), p. 99.

Table 28. Mean coital frequency for non-sterile women as reported at second and third interviews, wife's age at third interview, and interval between second and third interviews, by current method of contraception

Method	Mean monthly coital frequency			Wife's age	Interval in years	Number
	Second interview	Third interview	Percent change			
Total	7.0	6.2	-11	35.7	5.4	689
Effective	7.0	6.6	- 5	35.7	5.3	391
Other than effective	7.0	5.7	-18	35.7	5.5	298

achieve their desired number. In short, particularly for women using effective methods, the major portion of increased contraceptive efficiency must derive from more faithful use of these methods.

While this analysis has been concerned with the effect of declining rates of coital frequency on contraceptive efficacy, the results indicate that the effectiveness of a contraceptive method may in turn affect coital frequency. This question has recently received attention with respect to the oral contraceptives.

The Pill and Coital Frequency[7]

Although it is possible that the various side effects of the pill are common enough to decrease sexual activity, the opposite point of view is usually suggested in the literature on this subject. There are several reasons why the adoption of this modern method might result in a significant increase

[7] This section summarizes parts of Charles F. Westoff, Larry Bumpass, and Norman B. Ryder, "Oral Contraception, Coital Frequency, and the Time Required to Conceive," *Social Biology 16*, No. 1 (1969): 1-10.

in marital sexual activity: 1) the reduction of anxiety about pregnancy removes a potentially serious impairment of coital activity; 2) the physical separation of contraception from the sexual act may increase spontaneity and enjoyment; 3) the biochemical action of the progesterone component of the pill may increase female libido.

The evidence thus far assembled on this question has been inconclusive, either because of small or unrepresentative samples or because of various methodological limitations complicating the analysis, such as the absence of "before" and "after" measurement or the lack of an adequate control group.

The 1965 National Fertility Study reports an 18-20 percent difference in coital frequency between women using the pill and women using other contraceptive methods.[8] While this difference persists by education, age, and religion, it is impossible to rule out selectivity when treating this kind of question with cross-sectional data: couples with higher rates of coital frequency may be more likely than those with lower rates to select the pill because of its unobtrusiveness. The plausibility of our inference about the effect of the pill would be greatly improved if we had a "before" and "after" report of women who did and who did not adopt the pill. Our longitudinal study provides such data.

The comparisons of interest are those between the coital frequency rates of 69 women before and after they began using the pill (1960 and 1963-67 respectively) and those between the rates at comparable times for the 354 women who used other methods. Since the pill is used more by younger women, who normally have a higher average coital frequency even within this relatively homogeneous group aged 30-39, we calculated a rate standardized on the age distribution of women using the pill in order to control any effect of age on the comparison of the two categories of women.

The main observations from Table 29 are: 1) a 5 percent

[8] *Loc. cit.*

Table 29. Mean coital frequencies reported by women interviewed before and after use of the pill and other contraceptive methods

Method reported in third interview	Number of women	Mean monthly coital frequency		Percent change
		1960	1963-67	
Pill	69	7.1	7.5	+5
Other methods	354	7.2	6.5	-10
Other methods (standardized)[a]	354	7.4	6.6	-11

[a]Standardized on the age distribution of women using the pill.

increase in mean coital frequency over the 5 to 6 years for women who used the pill; 2) a 10 percent *decrease* over the same time period for women who used other methods of contraception; 3) no evidence that women with an initially high frequency were attracted to the pill. Using the *t* test for the significance of differences between means, and given the small number of users, the change in frequency among women using the pill is not large enough to be statistically significant; but the decrease among women using other methods is significant at the .001 level. Prior to the use of the pill, the difference between the mean frequencies for the two categories of women is 0.1 in the opposite direction and not statistically significant, but at reinterview the difference is 1.0 in the predicted direction and significant at the .02 level.

It seems clear from this analysis that the pill does make a difference in coital frequency and that the 1965 National Fertility Study report of an 18-20 percent difference in frequency between users and non-users among women aged 25-44 is quite consistent with the difference between the rate for women in our study of comparable age using the pill (7.5) and the rate they theoretically might have had (6.3)[9] if they had not shifted to the pill. It is quite

[9] This hypothetical rate was estimated by applying the 11 percent

impossible from these data and this type of study to determine the relative importance of social, psychological, or biochemical factors in causing this difference.

Summary and Conclusions

The use of contraception and the effectiveness with which it is used are closely tied to the number of children a woman wants to have. The vast majority of the women who did not use contraception before their first birth wanted to have at least three children. After the second child is born virtually all women use contraception, but the effectiveness of their use varies markedly depending upon whether or not they want an additional child. After achieving the number of children they desire, some couples turn to sterilization as a way of preventing unwanted births; others use contraception more effectively. In sum, these data add to the accumulating body of evidence that family-planning control is much more salient for women when they are seeking to prevent births than when they merely wish to delay them, and that failure rates observed in a cross-section of a population are not necessarily indicative of the population's ability to avoid excess fertility.

While demonstrating the relationship of fertility control to desired family size, these data also reflect on the nature of desired family size as a predictive variable. We have seen in an earlier chapter that at the aggregate level, within religion and education controls, average completed family size is *very* close to the number of children desired some 8 years earlier. The data reported in this chapter lend further support to the thesis that this correspondence is not fortuitous. Sharp differences in contraceptive performance after the second birth between groups defined on the basis of the number of children they desired *at the time* of the second birth indicate that the number of children desired at a point in time is a goal in terms of which couples regulate their subsequent behavior.

decrease for the standardized means of the women using other methods to the mean of 7.1 for women who subsequently adopted the pill.

VI · Social and Psychological Influences on Fertility

Over the three decades since the Indianapolis Study, concern with the social and psychological determinants of fertility has remained a major theme in American fertility research. This chapter continues this interest in social and psychological influences. Socioeconomic differences in fertility are considered briefly along with an examination of the way in which a parity-specific sample complicates such an analysis. Throughout this study we have utilized the fact that religion is an important variable in the family-building process, and we summarize those differences here. In addition we consider in this chapter the relation of fertility to peer-group relations, wife's work, size of parental family, sex of offspring, and a number of attitudes and psychological orientations. The question of the relationship between fertility and patterns of socioeconomic mobility is treated separately in Chapter VII.

Socioeconomic Differentials in Fertility: The Methodological Problem

Since socioeconomic differentials in fertility have long been considered an important aspect of the study of fertility,[1] the lack of an extensive treatment of such differentials in this volume warrants explanation. While the design of this study is propitious for the kinds of analyses we have undertaken, it is problematic for the study of differential fertility. In general this is true because of the way in which a parity-specific sample intersects a common

[1] For example, Charles F. Westoff, "Differential Fertility in the United States: 1900-1952," *American Sociological Review* 29, No. 5 (1954): 549-61; Clyde V. Kiser, "Differential Fertility in the United States," in National Bureau of Economic Research, *Demographic and Economic Change in Developed Countries* (Princeton: Princeton University Press, 1960); David Goldberg, "Fertility and Fertility Differentials: Some Observations on Recent Changes in the United States," *Public Health and Population Change*, Mindel C. Sheps and Jeanne Clare Ridley, eds. (Pittsburgh: University of Pittsburgh Press, 1965).

point for all respondents with respect to fertility while simultaneously intersecting respondents at varying points with respect to other life-cycle variables.

The problem is clearest with respect to income or occupation. Women who were older at the birth of their second child were generally married to older husbands. Consequently the income and occupation reported for these couples represents a later stage in the socioeconomic life-cycle than that reported for couples who were younger at the birth of their second child. At the same time the older couples are likely to have fewer additional births than the younger couples—as a consequence of the selected attitudes and the differences in fertility planning and fecundity which resulted in their long birth intervals, as well as because of their shorter remaining risk period before infertility. The result of this selectivity is a bias in cross-sectional analysis towards a negative association of socioeconomic variables and fertility. This bias is least problematic for education, since education is a fixed characteristic for most women by the time their second child is born. Consequently, attention should be focused on the relationship between education and fertility, although the correlations with occupation and income are also included in Table 30.[2]

[2] The fact that the correlations of fertility with occupation and income parallel those of fertility and education indicates that the biases arising from a parity-specific sample may not be as serious as they could be. On the other hand, there are changes over the time period studied in the correlations of fertility with income and occupation which may or may not be a product of the study design. Between 1956 and 1963-67 these correlations become less negative for Protestants and more positive for Catholics. Taken at face value these patterns might imply that the time perspective of family building also varies by religion—that is, that for Protestants the relevant economic status for family building is that which exists early in childbearing while for Catholics the relevant economic status is that which they expect to achieve ultimately. However, it is more likely that these differences are a product of the bias in our data towards negative status differentials. Such a bias would be strongest with respect to the 1959 data because age differences are minimized at the third interview through the interviewing design in which older women were interviewed first (see Chapter I). The net result of a stronger

Table 30. Correlations between fertility and socioeconomic variables, by religion

Socioeconomic variable	Total	Protestant			Catholic			Jewish
		All	Active	Other	All	Active	Other	
Wife's education	-.01	-.13	-.04	-.19	.18	.20	.09	.16
Husband's income								
1956	-.15	-.27	-.22	-.30	-.02	.05	-.08	.06
1959	-.08	-.19	-.16	-.21	.06	.13	-.01	.13
1962-66	.04	-.03	.09	-.11	.18	.27	.10	.09
Husband's occupational prestige								
1956	-.04	-.14	-.09	-.16	.11	.09	.06	.21
1959	-.02	-.13	-.03	-.18	.15	.18	.09	.17
1962-66	.04	-.06	.06	-.13	.21	.34	.12	.13
Number of women	814	333	136	197	383	95	288	98

Differential Fertility

While socioeconomic differentials in fertility can be considered for their implications for differential growth rates, it is clear that there is no simple additive "effect" of status on fertility. A substantial literature reports that socioeconomic differentials in fertility depend upon religion.[3] In these analyses it has been customary to classify women by religion as Catholic or non-Catholic, largely because of the small number of Jewish women in most samples. These studies report that fertility is related to status inversely for non-Catholics but directly for Catholics; and this difference is generally attributed to the different "meaning" of status in the Catholic and non-Catholic contexts. It is asserted that for non-Catholics "secularism" of role patterns is directly related to socioeconomic status, while among Catholics the obverse is true primarily because Catholics who have attended college are also likely to be those who are most committed to the teachings of the Church on familial values and contraceptive use.

The relationship of fertility to socioeconomic status depends also on the wife's age at marriage.[4] The strong negative relationship observed when the wife's age at marriage is young diminishes with advancing age at marriage and becomes positive for wives who married at older ages. Since this is true for Catholics as well as for non-Catholics, it has been suggested that the observed difference between Catholics and non-Catholics in the status-fertility relationship is to some extent a product of the fact that Catholics

---

negative bias for the 1956 than for the 1963-66 measurements would be to reinforce negative differentials while "washing out" positive relationships in the earlier measurement.

[3] Westoff, Potter, and Sagi, *The Third Child*, pp. 108-121; Ronald Freedman, David Goldberg, and Larry Bumpass, "Current Fertility Expectations of Married Couples in the United States: 1963," *Population Index* 31 (1965): 13; Goldberg, "Fertility and Fertility Differentials," p. 139; Whelpton, Campbell, and Patterson, *Fertility and Family Planning*, pp. 96-106.

[4] Larry Bumpass, "Age at Marriage as a Variable in Socioeconomic Differentials in Fertility," *Demography* 6, No. 1 (1969): 45-54.

marry at older ages than do non-Catholics—i.e., at the ages for which socioeconomic status is positively related to fertility for all religious groups.

The metropolitan composition of our sample permits separate analysis for Jewish women, and the result lends support to the above thesis that much of the religious interaction may be attributable to religious differences in age at marriage. Table 30 presents the correlations between status variables and fertility. As reported in other studies, the correlations are negative for Protestants but positive for Catholics. It is instructive to note, however, that the correlations are also positive among Jewish women. Attempts to explain the religious interaction in terms of religious differences in the "meaning" of status variables with respect to secularism ought to take into account the similarity between Catholics and Jews in this respect. This similarity seems most readily understandable if we interpret the religious interaction with the status-fertility relationship in terms of differences by religion in age at marriage. Jewish women, as well as Catholic women, tend to marry at the older ages where status is related positively to fertility, while Protestants tend to marry at the younger ages where status is related inversely to fertility.

It is suggested elsewhere that both selective fecundity and the incidence of nonfamilial adult roles among low-status women vary by age at marriage and underlie the observed interaction by age at marriage in the status-fertility relationship.[5] A tendency for religious groups to marry at different ages could lead to socioeconomic differentials in fertility which differ in direction by religion (as those observed here) in the absence of religious differences with respect to the *process* of differential fertility. This is not to suggest that there are no differences between Catholics and Protestants in orientation toward social status independent of age at marriage, but only that these differences may not contribute much to differences in the status-fertility relationship.

[5] *Ibid.*

Religion and Religiosity

It has become increasingly clear in American fertility research that religion is an important variable affecting the family-building process. The fact that on the average Catholic women both desire and have larger families than non-Catholic women has now been documented repeatedly by sample surveys.[6] In addition much attention has recently been drawn to the Roman Catholic Church's official doctrine on contraception and the resulting dissension among the Catholic clergy and laity.[7] The longitudinal nature of our study provides an excellent opportunity for comparing religious differences not only with respect to completed family size but also with respect to the various aspects of the family-building process.

Degree of Religious Commitment

Virtually all Americans identify themselves with one of the three major religious groups in the United States. For many this is a nominal identification; for others, it is a commitment to a particular community of beliefs. Consequently, the effects of religious beliefs on fertility behavior may be understated if variations in commitment are ignored. Listed below are the criteria we used in the attempt to distinguish those who are "actively" identified with either the Protestant or the Catholic faith. Jewish couples have not been subclassified on degree of commitment because of the small number of Jews in our sample.

Active Protestants (136 couples):

1. Married by a minister

[6] Freedman, Whelpton, and Campbell, *Family Planning*, pp. 277-87; Whelpton, Campbell, and Patterson, *Fertility and Family Planning*, pp. 69-93; Freedman and Bumpass, "Fertility Expectations," pp. 191-94; Norman B. Ryder and Charles F. Westoff, *Report of the 1965 National Fertility Study* (Princeton University Press, 1971).

[7] For a detailed analysis of the effect of the Papal Encyclical on Catholic conformity, see Charles F. Westoff and Norman B. Ryder, "The Papal Encyclical and Catholic Practice and Attitudes: United States, 1969," *Studies in Family Planning* (February, 1969).

2. Both spouses report Protestant identification at all three interviews.
3. The reported frequency of church attendance at all three interviews is more often than once a year for the husband and at least once a month for the wife.

Other Protestants (197 couples):
All others who were classified as Protestant at the first interview, including all mixed marriages not married by a priest.

Active Catholics (95 couples):
1. Married by a priest
2. Both spouses received at least some education in Catholic schools.
3. Both spouses reported Catholic identification at all three interviews.
4. The reported frequency of church attendance is at least once a week for both spouses at all three interviews.

Other Catholics (288 couples):
All others who were classified as Catholic at the first interview.

Changes in Religious Identification and Attendance

As implied in the above religious classification there are changes in religious identification and church attendance over the study period. Tables 31 and 32 compare these characteristics at the first and third interviews. Over 95 percent of the respondents in each of the major groups reported the same identification at the first and third interviews. Some of the changes occurred to individuals in original Protestant-Catholic marriages; others may reflect unreliability of measurement. It is of interest that four-fifths of the individuals who reported no religion at the first interview identify with one of the three major groups at the third. This suggests a tendency for religious identifica-

Table 31. Religious identification at first interview, by religious identification at third interview

First interview	Third interview					Total	
	P	C	J	O	N	%	N
Wife's religion							
Protestant	95	2	--	2	1	100	326
Catholic	3	95	--	0	2	100	368
Jewish	1	--	99	--	--	100	94
Other	12	6	--	81	--	100	16
Nothing	*	*	*	--	--	100	9
Husband's religion							
Protestant	95	2	--	1	2	100	308
Catholic	4	94	--	0	2	100	366
Jewish	2	--	96	--	2	100	95
Other	26	--	--	68	5	100	19
Nothing	44	12	16	--	28	100	25

*Base less than 10 sample cases

-- Zero frequency

0 less than .05 percent

Table 32. Frequency of church attendance at first and third interviews for husbands and wives

Frequency of attendance	Husbands, by interview		Wives, by interview	
	1st	3rd	1st	3rd
Weekly	39	44	43	56
1 - 3 per month	17	15	20	20
More than 1 per year	25	23	24	16
1 per year or less	18	18	13	8
Total: Percent	100	100	100	100
Number	814	814	814	814

tion to increase with age, and Table 32 further supports this idea. For both spouses, but particularly for wives, there is a shift toward more frequent church attendance over the years.

Fertility Differences by Religion

Because of the importance of religion to fertility, we have employed religion as a control variable in most of the analyses reported in this volume. The major conclusions concerning religious differences will be summarized briefly here. As reported in other studies, Catholics desire and achieve the largest families and Jewish women desire and achieve the smallest families (Table 33). It has frequently been noted that the effect of Catholicism on fertility behavior is strongly influenced by the degree of commitment to the Catholic community. This is illustrated in our data by the fact that Other Catholics are more similar to Protestants with respect to desired and achieved family size than they are to Active Catholics.[8] The close similarity of

[8] Similar results are reported by Westoff and Ryder, *ibid.*

Table 33. Mean number of children desired at first interview
and mean completed parity, by religion

Religion	Mean desired	Mean completed parity	Number of couples
Total	3.3	3.3	814
Protestant	3.0	3.0	333
Active	3.1	3.0	136
Other	2.9	3.0	197
Catholic	3.6	3.6	383
Active	4.3	4.3	95
Other	3.4	3.4	288
Jewish	2.7	2.6	98

Active and Other Protestants in most of our analyses suggests that with respect to fertility behavior the designation "Protestant" denotes a group of women who are neither Catholic nor Jewish more than it specifies a particular set of beliefs relevant to fertility.

As illustrated in Table 33, the religious categories are very similar with respect to the agreement between average family size desired at the first interview and that finally achieved; for all groups there is nearly complete aggregate correspondence (see Chapter IV). However, Jewish women are most likely to achieve the number they initially wanted and Catholic women least likely. For over one-quarter of the Active Catholics, completed family size differs by two or more children from the number originally desired—but these women are as likely to have fewer as to have more children than originally desired.

83

Women who have larger families space their children more closely than do women with smaller families. Since Catholics achieve larger families than non-Catholics, each birth interval is, on the average, shorter among Catholics. However, an analysis reported in Chapter III indicates that this fact ought not to be interpreted as indicating that shorter birth intervals are a result of any Catholic values independent of the achievement of large families. When the average interval between marriage and the last child has been standardized on the total parity distribution,[9] it is *longer* for Catholics (108 months) than for non-Catholics (104 months).

Catholic–non-Catholic differentials in contraceptive use and efficacy early in the family-building process are inflated by the fact that Catholics are further from the point in time at which they will face the risk of an unwanted birth. By the third interview Catholics are much more similar to Protestants with respect to extent of use and methods of contraception than they were at the first interview. Jewish women are most likely to use contraception and to use effective methods of contraception at all points in the family-building process.

Although there are differences between Catholics and non-Catholics in the methods of contraception used, there is little difference between the two groups in efficacy of fertility control after motivation to control fertility, as inferred from the number of children desired, is taken into account (see Chapter V).

We have noted that as women achieve the number of children they desire and face the task of preventing unwanted births, there is an increased tendency to use contraception and to use the more effective methods. An interesting question not raised earlier in this volume is whether Catholic women who change from rhythm or nonuse to methods not approved by the Church reduce their

---

[9] Women of seven or higher parity are excluded since there are no non-Catholic women at these parities in our sample. Three percent of the Catholic women have borne seven or more children.

frequency of church attendance in order to minimize dissonance between their behavior and official church doctrine, or conversely, whether those whose religious commitment declines are more likely to adopt disapproved methods. Among Catholic women who did not use methods disapproved by the Church prior to the first interview, a shift to effective methods of contraception is negatively correlated with both religious-mindedness and frequency of church attendance at both the first and third interviews, but is uncorrelated with a change in these variables (Table 34). In other words, among Catholic women using

Table 34. Correlations between measures of religiosity and the adoption of effective contraceptive methods (dichotomized), for 139 Catholic women who used only Church approved methods before both their first and second births

Item	First interview	Third interview	Increase first to third
Religious mindedness	-.25	-.20	-.04
Frequency of church attendance	-.30	-.28	-.06

Church-approved methods, those who are less committed to the Church are more likely to adopt effective methods of contraception in the future, but women who adopt the more effective methods do not reduce their frequency of church attendance or degree of religious-mindedness, nor are women whose church attendance declines more likely to adopt disapproved methods.

Characteristics of Friends

If childbearing constitutes one of the most salient aspects of the female role for women in our society, then it is likely to be influenced by the primary group. On the basis of the Indianapolis Study, Potter and Kantner report a correlation of .4 between a woman's family size and the average family size of her three closest friends.[10] They note that the basis for such a relationship may be twofold. On the one hand, closest friends may be the most likely persons to influence a woman's values about family size. On the other hand, selection of friends may occur on the basis of similar family sizes. Most commonly such selection probably differentiates between childless couples and couples with children, but it may also operate between couples with very small or very large families because of child-care considerations, types of recreation that are feasible, and similar factors. At the same time, such selectivity may result simply from homogeneous residential aggregations of houses of a certain size. The authors note that since the correlation between family sizes of respondents and friends is no lower among respondents with unwanted births than among "efficient planners," the relationship may be largely a product of selectivity rather than influence.

A few questions relating to this discussion were asked in the present study. In some ways our data are more appropriate for this purpose than those of the Indianapolis Study. Selectivity involving childless women is excluded as a result of the sample design. In addition, estimated completed fertility is obtained both for the respondents and for their friends, minimizing variation resulting from the fact that friends may be at different stages of the life-cycle at the time of interview.

The four characteristics of friends considered here are: estimated completed family size, relationship to the respondent, membership in Catholic Church, and income relative to respondent. The results in Table 35 agree surprisingly with those of Potter and Kantner's study, given the differences in sample and procedure. The respondent's

[10] Robert G. Potter, Jr., and John F. Kantner, "The Influence of Siblings and Friends on Fertility," *Milbank Memorial Fund Quarterly* 33, No. 3 (1955): 246-67.

Table 35. Correlations between completed family size of the respondent and characteristics of her three closest friends

| Group | Correlation between respondent's completed family size and: | | | | |
	Average family size	Proportion of friends relatives	Proportion of friends Catholic	Relative income	Number of women
Total	.36	.00	.25	.03	814
Protestant	.14	.02	-.02	-.01	333
Active	.16	.06	-.02	-.02	136
Other	.13	.00	-.03	-.00	197
Catholic	.37	-.08	.16	.08	383
Active	.31	-.14	.08	.25	95
Other	.35	-.05	.11	-.05	288
Jewish	.30	-.18	.20	-.04	98
Mean association time:					
Under 12 years	.36	-.08	.36	.06	356
12 years or more	.38	-.04	.35	.05	458

family size correlates .36 with the mean family size of friends. Since fertility differs quite strongly by religion, one possible source of this correlation is the religious similarity of friends. The correlation remains within religious groups, although it is higher among Catholics and Jews than among Protestants.

The prevalence of relatives among a wife's friends may influence how traditional she is in her life style and family-building patterns. In general we expect kinship ties to be associated with higher fertility, but, of course, this is true only when such traditions involve high fertility patterns. In these data the proportion of the three closest friends who are relatives is associated with the respondent's family size only among Active Catholics and Jews—in both cases the correlation is negative. These are the subgroups for which distinct traditions are likely to exist, and the negative influence of relatives on family size among Jewish women is consistent with the low fertility of the Jewish community. However, that this relationship is also negative among Active Catholics appears anomalous.

Protestants who have Catholic friends do not differ in their fertility from other Protestants, but Catholics with Protestant friends have slightly lower fertility than other Catholics.

Only among Active Catholics is there a correlation between fertility and the relative income of friends. The "better off" Active Catholics feel, compared with their friends, the larger is their family size.

These relationships could be influenced by how long a wife has known her friends. The friends reported on are current friends and very well may not be those who were most influential in the earlier stages of childbearing and the formation of values about family size. There is, however, little difference when we compare the correlations between women who have known the friends reported on for less than 12 years and those who have known these friends for 12 years or more.

The Potter and Kantner study compared "efficient" and "inefficient" planners on the assumption that any influence of friends would be most evident among women who had not experienced an unwanted birth. However, the effect of primary group influence on fertility values is diluted for planners as well as for non-planners through differential fecundities—to some extent the subfecund (women who cannot achieve the number they want) are concentrated among planners. On the other hand, attitudes toward contraceptive practice may be an important aspect of primary

88

group influence on fertility (particularly among Catholics). One approach to this question from our data is to examine the relation between family-size desires at the first interview and the average completed family size of friends. The number of children desired at the first interview was reported before experience with subfecundity or unwanted births for most women, and yet it shows a correlation of .28 with the average fertility of friends.

As indicated at the beginning of this section, it would seem strange indeed if close friends exerted no influence at all on one of the most important aspects of a woman's role in our society. The task of uncovering the dynamics of that (reciprocal) influence is very complex and requires more sensitive measures and a more thorough approach than have been brought to bear on this question to date.

Size of Parental Family

Several studies have considered the relationship between the size of family of orientation and marital fertility.[11] The evidence concerning the existence of such a relationship is conflicting, but the larger and more general samples indicate that size of parental family exercises a modest, though demographically significant, effect on marital fertility. Such an effect may operate at three levels. First, it is possible that differences in fecundity are inherited, although this factor should not be of major significance in a contracepting population. Second, some selectivity with respect to the length of exposure to risk of pregnancy may be associated with size of parental family. Women from large

[11] Sven Moberg, "Marital Status and Family Size among Matriculated Persons in Sweden," *Population Studies* 4 (1950): 115-27; Jerzy Berent, "Relationships between Family Size of Two Successive Generations," *Milbank Memorial Fund Quarterly* 31 (1953): 39-50; John F. Kantner and Robert G. Potter, Jr., "Social and Psychological Factors Affecting Fertility: XXIV. The Relationship of Family Size in Two Successive Generations," *Milbank Memorial Fund Quarterly* 32 (1954): 294-311; Otis Dudley Duncan, Ronald Freedman, J. Michael Coble, and Doris P. Slesinger, "Marital Fertility and the Size of Family of Orientation," *Demography* 2 (1965): 508-15.

families leave school at an early age, marry young, and begin childbearing at an early age.[12] Finally, individuals may attempt to create in their own family an environment similar to the one in which they were reared. Norms about family size are probably learned in much the same way as other norms and values.[13] In addition there may be less conscious pressures toward intergenerational similarity in family size.

The role relationships in the family of orientation will depend partly on the number of persons in that family; hence any tendency to recapitulate these relationships will induce a tendency to reproduce a family of similar size.[14]

Duncan, Freedman, Coble, and Slesinger extended the understanding of this effect by demonstrating how it is mediated by differential exposure (particularly as picked up through education differentials) for the population at large; while at the same time finding that among "fecund planners" the size of the parental family exerts a direct effect upon fertility largely independent of education or marriage duration.[15] The purpose of the present analysis is to add to previous studies by examining this effect among the couples in our study, and by considering how it may vary by religion.

The relation of completed fertility to number of siblings is lower in our data than in the Growth of American Family data reported by Duncan et al. We find a regression coefficient of .04 (Table 36), while they report a coefficient of .08. One important reason for this difference is the fact that since our sample is originally drawn from second parity women, a potentially important source of variance in completed family size is lost through the exclusion of childless and one-child families. Consequently our sample does

[12] Duncan, et al., *ibid.*, 514.
[13] Charles F. Westoff, *College Women and Fertility Values* (Princeton: Princeton University Press, 1967), pp. 122-23.
[14] Duncan, et al., "Marital Fertility," 514.
[15] *Loc. cit.*

90

Table 36. Regression of completed parity and number of children desired at first interview on number of wife's siblings, by religion and happiness of childhood

Regression on number of wife's siblings of:

Sample	Completed parity				Desired family size			
	Net of wife's:				Net of wife's:			
	Gross	Educ.	Mar. age	Educ. and mar. age	Gross	Educ.	Mar. age	Educ. and mar. age
Total	.04	.04	.04	.06	.06	.07	.06	.09
Protestant:	.07	.05	.05	.05	.06	.07	.05	.07
Active	.09	.09	.07	.09	.08	.07	.10	.10
Other	.06	.04	.03	.04	.05	.05	.04	.05
Catholic:	-.04	-.01	-.04	.00	.00	.04	.00	.05
Active	-.13	-.10	-.12	-.06	-.03	.04	-.02	.06
Other	.00	.01	.00	.02	.02	.03	.02	.04
Jewish	-.04	-.02	.02	.04	-.05	-.03	-.04	.00
Childhood:								
Happy	.02	.05	.02	.06	.07	.11	.07	.11
Mixed	.08	.07	.09	.09	.08	.09	.08	.10
Unhappy	-.02	-.02	-.03	-.01	.02	.04	.02	.04

not permit us to speak to the absolute size of this relationship in the population at large. Nevertheless there are
some intriguing differences by religion and happiness of
childhood which warrant examination.

Among Protestants there is, as expected, a modest positive effect of the number of siblings on fertility. The fact
that this effect is as strong on the number of children desired at the first interview as it is on the number finally
achieved indicates that selective involuntary factors are not
likely to have played a major role in the establishing of
this relationship.

On the other hand, the expected relationships do not obtain among Catholics or Jews. The size of the parental
family is negatively related to fertility among both Active
Catholics and Jews. It was noted early in this chapter
that for these groups fertility is directly related to education. This being the case, the negative effect of the number
of siblings on fertility observed here could result from the
negative relation between size of parental family and educational attainment. After adjustments have been made for
the effects of education and age at marriage, the regression
coefficient becomes positive for Jewish women and is reduced to —.06 among Active Catholics. It is not implausible
that this remaining negative relationship results from the
intergenerational increase in fertility experienced by Active
Catholics. Among this group, those who come from smaller
families may have responded most to the economic and social conditions conducive to higher fertility.

It has been suggested elsewhere that the effect of parental family size on one's own family size depends upon
whether one's early experience was satisfying.[16] Consistent
with this, family-size desires at the birth of the second
child are directly related to parental family size for all
couples except those reporting an unhappy childhood.[17] In

[16] Westoff, Potter, Sagi, and Mishler, *Family Growth*, p. 292.
[17] For wives with a happy childhood the correlation between number of children desired by the wife and number of the wife's siblings
is .10, not —.11, erroneously reported in *Family Growth*, p. 292.

92

the gross relationships, completed fertility is related to parental family size only among these reporting intermediate happiness of childhood. However after the effects of education and age at marriage have been taken into account it is true for completed fertility as well as for desired fertility, that the effect of parental family size is positive (though small) for all but those reporting an unhappy childhood.

Duncan et al. report that "there is no evidence for the greater importance of the number of siblings of the wife as compared to the husband."[18] Our data confirm this in that for the total sample the regression coefficient for the husband's siblings is comparable to that for the wife's siblings and neither is altered when both are included in a multiple regression equation.

Sex of Offspring

The number of children a couple wishes to have may be conditional upon the sex composition of the family. Evidence was presented in the first volume of this series that the number of children desired after the second birth varied systematically with the sex composition of the first two children, and *The Third Child* reports that fertility during the subsequent 3-year period was consistent with this variation in desires.[19]

Table 37 demonstrates that when the women in our sample have reached completed fertility, the desire to have at least one child of each sex has indeed influenced the number of children born. Births of a third, fourth, and even fifth order are more likely to occur if the preceding births were all of the same sex. Considering the parity progression ratios for the third birth (where the number of cases is most susbtantial), couples whose first two children were boys are 11 percent more likely to have another child than are couples whose first two children included a child of each sex; if the first two children were girls the prob-

18 Duncan, et al., "Marital Fertility," p. 514.
19 Westoff, Potter, and Sagi, *The Third Child*, pp. 205-207.

Table 37. Comparison of parity progression ratios by sex composition of preceding births

| Sex composition of preceding births | Parity progression ratio | | Number of cases |
	Actual	Standardized on "mixed"	
Third birth			
All boys	.69	1.11	221
Mixed	.62	1.00	389
All girls	.77	1.24	193
Fourth birth			
All boys	.62	1.10	68
Mixed	.48	1.00	405
All girls	.50	1.04	68
Fifth birth			
All one sex	.58	1.36	33
Mixed	.42	1.00	218

ability of a third birth is 24 percent higher than if there was a child of each sex. At the extreme, among couples with four children all of the same sex, the probability of having a fifth birth is 36 percent greater than for couples whose four children include both sexes.

Wife's Work

Whether or not the wife is working often stands out as one of the strongest predictors of fertility in cross-sectional analyses.[20] However, the causal ordering of this relation-

[20] For example, Freedman and Bumpass, "Current Fertility Expectations," p. 194.

ship is not at all clear. Do women limit their fertility in order to have time to pursue their non-family-oriented interests, or do women work if their fertility permits them to do so?[21] The one piece of evidence that may be usefully brought to bear from our longitudinal data is the predictability of early work orientation for completed fertility.

Our first measure of orientation toward work occurs at an identical point in the childbearing cycle for all women in our sample—6 months after the birth of their second child. Women were ordered on the basis of their orientation toward work ranging from those who were currently

Table 38. Intercorrelations among measures of the wife's orientation toward work at each of the three interviews and correlations between these variables and completed family size

| Wife's orientation toward work | Wife's orientation toward work at interview: | | | Completed family size |
	1	2	3	
Summary index	.74	.83	.77	-.12
Interviews: 1	--	.48	.33	-.08
2		--	.42	-.08
3			--	-.13

employed to those who did not expect to work in the future. Similar measures were derived from the second and third interviews.

The relationship between a wife's orientation toward

[21] An excellent analysis of the complexity of this multidirectional influence can be found in James A. Sweet, "Family Composition and the Labor Force Activity of Married Women in the United States," Ph.D. dissertation, University of Michigan, 1968.

work immediately after the birth of her second child and her completed fertility is very weak, although it is in the predicted direction. The selective nature of the influence of fertility on the employment of wives is suggested by the fact that orientation towards work as measured at the third interview correlates more highly with completed fertility than either of the preceding measures. As women near the end of their childbearing, those with the smaller families are freed earlier from childbearing responsibilities and consequently are able to enter the labor force.

Attitudinal and Personality Measures

One of the ambitious undertakings of this study at its inception over a decade ago was the measurement of certain attitudes and personality characteristics through interviews in an attempt to relate such variables to fertility.

It seems reasonable that the interests and attitudes a woman brings into marriage, as well as her basic personality characteristics, should condition the emphasis she places upon the mother role vis-à-vis other adult female roles. Emphasis on the mother role may, of course, be reflected in the intensity of child care as well as the number of children born, but it was hypothesized that fertility itself would be affected.

The measurement of and rationale for these variables is described fully in the first volume of this study. [22] Briefly, the attitudinal variables are of two types. First, there are the measures directly concerned with family relationships: the wife's adjustment to the mother role, whether or not she thinks children are most enjoyable as babies, her liking for children, the availablility of help for child-care, her marital adjustment and the happiness of her own childhood. A second dimension assumed to be relevant to the emphasis placed on the mother role is the wife's orientation to socioeconomic achievement. Presumably a high social-status orientation would lead to a lesser interest in

[22] Westoff, Potter, Sagi, and Mishler, *Family Growth*, pp. 30, 175-77, 316-19.

96

Table 39. Correlations of completed family size with family-related attitudes, by religion

Variable	Total	Protes-tants	Cath-olics	Jews	Protestants		Catholics	
					Active	Other	Active	Other
Adjustment to mother role	.04	.02	.06	.02	.12	-.04	.07	.05
Children most enjoyable when babies	-.05	-.09	-.05	-.06	-.06	-.11	-.08	-.02
Liking for children	.04	.02	.00	.10	.04	.02	.06	-.04
Help available for child-care	.03	-.01	.05	.18	.07	-.06	-.02	.10
Marital adjustment	.03	.02	.06	.09	.07	.00	.17	-.01
Happiness of childhood	.00	-.02	.02	.08	.07	-.08	.06	-.04

the mother role and to lower fertility. (The theory of the relation between fertility and status mobility is considered more fully in the following chapter.) A large number of questions were asked in the attempt to measure social status orientation, including: whether the wife felt she was achieving her life goals, how economically secure she felt, how satisfied she was with her husband's job, her perception of her husband's opportunities to get ahead, her aspirations for her children's education, her drive to get ahead, how willing she was to sacrifice convictions and social interests in order to get ahead, whether she perceived the

Table 40. Correlations of completed family size with measures of wife's social status orientation, by religion

Variable	Total	Protes- tants	Catho- lics	Jews	Protestants Active	Other	Catholics Active	Other
Achievement of life goals	.05	-.06	.13	.11	-.01	-.08	.17	.06
Feelings of economic security	-.03	-.16	.05	.15	-.16	-.17	.04	.00
Satisfaction with husband's job	.01	-.10	.11	.05	-.04	-.13	.19	.07
Perception of husband's opportunities	.05	-.01	.14	.09	.16	-.11	.19	.08
College aspirations for children	.02	-.02	.13	-.23	.00	-.03	.26	.06
Drive to get ahead	-.04	.07	-.01	-.29	.15	.02	.18	-.06
Willingness to sacrifice convictions	-.07	.02	-.08	-.11	.08	-.03	-.12	-.02
Willingness to sacrifice social interests	-.04	.04	-.02	-.23	-.04	.10	-.09	.00
Perception of unfavorable effect of another child	-.04	.06	-.10	-.04	-.07	.15	-.08	-.06
Relevance of finances to having another	-.19	-.02	-.21	.05	.02	-.05	-.24	-.15
Tendency towards installment buying	.03	.14	-.12	.06	.05	.19	-.12	-.05
Social class identification	-.04	-.04	.04	-.08	.06	-.10	.10	-.04
Social class aspirations	-.04	-.04	.04	-.02	.12	-.13	-.06	.08
Social manners interest	-.03	-.09	.01	-.15	-.20	-.02	-.21	.10

effect of another child as unfavorable for getting ahead, the relevance of finances for having another child, how prone she was to buy on installment credit, her social class identification, her social class aspirations, and her interest in social manners. Social status orientations were also measured for the husbands in the mail questionnaire accompanying the first interview. Included among these were: willingness to sacrifice convictions in order to get ahead, feelings of economic security, commitment to work values, drive to get ahead, importance placed on getting ahead, and level of status satisfaction. Again the basic theme guiding the inclusion of these variables was that a drive for status is negatively associated with desires for children.

Table 41. Correlations of completed family size with measures of husband's attitudes, by religion

Variable	Total	Protes- tants	Cath- olics	Jews	Protestants Active	Other	Catholics Active	Other
Willingness to sacrifice convictions	-.04	-.05	.02	.01	.00	-.09	.15	-.02
Feelings of economic security	.01	-.04	.06	.02	-.04	-.03	.14	.01
Commitment to work values	.02	-.05	.13	.08	-.06	-.04	.19	.10
Drive to get ahead	-.07	.03	-.03	-.14	.06	.00	.10	-.05
Importance of getting ahead	.01	.08	-.05	-.02	.04	.10	-.02	-.04
Level of status satisfaction	.06	-.04	.21	.18	.00	-.06	.41	.09

Finally, it was hypothesized that certain types of personalities would be more consonant with the parental role than others. For example it seemed likely that obviously unsatisfied dependency needs and an immature concern for one's self and one's personal problems would reduce the desire for additional children. Variations in fertility control might well be related to the impulse-control balance established within the personality. After initial screening, the following personality measures were included in the study: generalized manifest anxiety, nurturance needs, ability to delay gratification of impulses, self-awareness, compulsiveness, ambiguity tolerance, preference for working alone, and need achievement. Scores on these characteristics were derived for wives from a mail questionnaire left after the first interview.

Table 42. Correlations of completed family size with measures of the wife's personality characteristics, by religion

Characteristics	Total	Protes- tants	Cath- olics	Jews	Protestants Active	Other	Catholics Active	Other
Manifest anxiety	-.03	-.04	-.05	-.06	-.07	-.03	-.06	-.01
Ambiguity tolerance	.07	.12	.09	.04	.10	.12	.09	.06
Impulse gratification	.00	.09	-.02	-.01	.20	.01	-.15	.05
Need achievement	.01	-.02	.02	-.13	-.05	.01	-.14	.06
Nurturance needs	-.01	-.01	.00	-.08	-.02	.00	.15	-.11
Work alone preference	-.02	-.06	.02	-.10	-.12	-.03	.05	-.04
Self-awareness	.02	-.04	.08	.10	-.04	-.04	.03	.04
Compulsiveness	-.04	-.04	-.08	-.00	-.16	.03	-.02	-.08

The correlations of these attitudinal and personality variables with completed fertility are presented in Tables 39-42. In all instances we are examining the association of the variable measured shortly after the birth of the second child with completed family size determined some 6-10 years later. The measures of various family relationships (Table 39) do not reveal associations with fertility of any magnitude or pattern. It seems strange, considering the plausibility of an association with fertility of such variables as "liking for children" or "adjustment to the mother role" that no relationships emerge.

The correlations of fertility with social status orientations

100

of both wives and husbands (Tables 40-41) also fail to provide any overwhelming support of our hypotheses. Here and there a few values appear impressive but caution must be exercised in view of the large number of correlations examined. In the total sample only the "relevance of finances" to fertility—a variable contaminated somewhat by the fact that the dependent variable is built into the question—shows any association. Looking at the religious subsamples, we see some evidence of a negative relation between mobility aspirations and fertility for Jews only. The only other pattern of interest is that in 19 of the 20 variables shown in Tables 40-41, the signs of the correlations are opposite for Protestants and Catholics, This, of course, is consistent with arguments presented elsewhere that the relation between life style and fertility varies by religion. It bears also on the probability that the reference groups involved in status orientations may differ markedly for Catholics and Protestants; among Catholics, the higher status groups are more involved with Catholicism which in turn implies higher fertility. Consistent with this interpretation is the fact that the correlations are higher for Active than for Other Catholics in 18 of the 20 comparisons. In general, higher fertility is positively associated with status orientations for Catholics and negatively associated for Protestants. While it is clear that there is a tendency for these measures to relate to fertility in opposite directions by religion, the magnitude of the relationships seems of little substantive significance.

In the first volume in this series, we undertook an analysis of the associations between various measures of the wife's personality characteristics and both the number of children desired after the second birth and the success with which the first two births had been planned. The results then were so discouraging that, except for a brief mention, the subject was not even included in the analysis reported in the second volume. At this final juncture of our study we felt some responsibility to check once more on the possibility that these personality variables might dis-

101

close some connections with fertility. We are now questioning whether the personality variables measured early in the reproductive history have any significance for completed size of family.

The results (Table 42) unfortunately do not provide any new bases for enthusiasm. None of the personality measures show any association with fertility at all for the total sample. Whether this failure to uncover such relationships is a reflection of measurement problems, or our failure to specify the conditions under which such relationships might hold, or simply a lack of validity of the theoretical premises is a continuing mystery about which we can only speculate.

Summary

This chapter is concerned with the effect on fertility of a number of social and psychological variables. In brief it reports that:

1) Parity specific samples pose serious methodological problems for the analysis of status differentials in fertility.

2) In general, fertility is related negatively to social status among Protestants, but positively among both Catholics and Jews.

3) Many of the differences by religion in birth spacing, contraceptive use, and contraceptive effectiveness, observed in cross-sectional data are attributable to differences in desired family size. Differences by religion in contraceptive behavior decline markedly after women have achieved the number of children they want.

4) There is a direct correlation between the respondent's family size and the family size of her three closest friends. Also examined are the effects on the respondent's fertility of other characteristics of her friends (their relation to her, their religion, and their income relative to hers), though no strong relationships are uncovered.

5) A positive correlation between fertility and the size of the parental family is found only for Protestants and for wives with a happy childhood.

6) Couples without children of both sexes are more likely to have an additional birth than couples who have at least one child of each sex.

7) A wife's orientation toward work after her second child is not highly predictive of her completed family size.

8) Analyses of the relationship of fertility to personality variables and to attitudinal variables concerned with family relationships and status orientations provide little encouragement for the use of these variables, at least as they are presently measured.

VII · Marital Fertility and the Process of Socioeconomic Achievement: An Examination of the Mobility Hypothesis[1]

BY DAVID L. FEATHERMAN

Princeton University

At the outset of the Princeton Fertility Study, one major research objective was the examination of the hypothesis that social mobility is directly related to family planning and inversely related to family size. This hypothesis can be traced to late nineteenth-century France and the writing of Arsène Dumont,[2] who argued the case for a mechanism of social mobility (*capillarité sociale*) by which small families have greater potential for upward mobility than do families of larger size. In a discussion of the mobility hypothesis, Blau and Duncan[3] distinguish between the "strong" versus the "weak" form of this conception. The strong form asserts "that differential fertility by socioeconomic status, social class, or some similar type of variable is completely explained by social mobility."[4] Blau and Duncan find no support for this form of the mobility hypothesis in their survey of the American male population in 1962, reporting that "occupational status makes at least as much difference in children ever born for the nonmobile as does occupational mobility for any stratum of origin (first job) or destination (current occupation)."[5]

The weak form of the mobility hypothesis posits that

[1] During the writing of this paper, the author was supported by a grant from the Manpower Administration of the U. S. Department of Labor pursuant to the provisions of the Manpower Development and Training Act of 1962. Reproduction in whole or in part is permitted for any purpose of the United States Government.

[2] Arsène Dumont, *Dépopulation et Civilisation* (Paris, 1890).

[3] Peter M. Blau and Otis Dudley Duncan, *The American Occupational Structure* (New York: John Wiley & Sons, 1967), p. 367.
    [4] *Loc. cit.*   [5] *Ibid.*, p. 374.

"social mobility, both in its subjective and objective dimensions, is directly related to fertility planning and inversely related to the size of the planned family—both relationships persisting in otherwise homogeneous socioeconomic groups."[6] This form of the hypothesis is consistent with the broad conceptual framework of the Princeton Fertility Study, although this study was originally couched in social psychological terms.[7] The line of reasoning behind the general hypotheses relating fertility and mobility has been stated succinctly by Westoff:

> Very briefly . . . the ideal-type of the couple either in the actual process of vertical mobility or effectively geared toward its anticipation probably has the following characteristics: a maintained rationality of behavior; intense competitive effort; careerism with its accompanying manipulation of personalities; psychological insecurity of status with its attendant anxieties; and an increasing exhaustion of nervous and physical energies; in short, a pervasive success-orientation and all that is implied by it.[8]

In this view, some psychological disposition (to be mobile) induces family limitation and (presumably) actual vertical mobility.

Existing data do not provide encouragement for the tenability of even the weak form of the mobility hypothesis. In the two earlier stages of this study,[9] no clear relationships were observed between changes in occupational or income statuses and actual fertility differentials in the total sample or among religious subgroups. For their cross-sec-

[6] Charles F. Westoff, "The Changing Focus of Differential Fertility Research: The Social Mobility Hypothesis," *Milbank Memorial Fund Quarterly* 31 (1953): 24-38; cited in Blau and Duncan, *ibid.*, p. 368.

[7] Westoff, Potter, Sagi, and Mishler, *Family Growth*, pp. 169-172.

[8] Westoff, as cited in Blau and Duncan, *Occupational Structure*, p. 369.

[9] Westoff, Potter, Sagi, and Mishler, *Family Growth*; Westoff, Potter, and Sagi, *The Third Child*.

tional data, Blau and Duncan report[10] some variation in completed family size which cannot be accounted for by a simple additive model including the effects of origin and destination occupational statuses. However, they find high mobility *in either direction* to be associated with smaller family sizes, with the fertility of mobile couples lying intermediate between that of couples remaining in the statuses of origin and that of nonmobile couples in the statuses of destination. These findings are difficult to reconcile with the mobility hypothesis as presently formulated.

The purpose of this chapter is to summarize, for the entire duration of the follow-up period (1957-67), the data that bear on the relationship between socioeconomic achievement and fertility. Two questions are involved. The first is whether couples who are psychologically oriented toward status mobility restrict their fertility accordingly. The second is whether fertility is in fact related to the process of objective mobility.

Achievement-Related Motivation and Subsequent Fertility

Suppose that the hypothesized relationship between fertility and mobility were rooted in some psychological disposition to be vertically mobile. Perhaps the *desire* to be upwardly mobile in the occupational and economic structures (rather than the actual movement itself) leads to the restriction of family size. Such a possible relationship has been advanced by Westoff and others who have rendered a more social psychological interpretation to the mobility hypothesis. In this formulation both fertility and actual socioeconomic achievements are taken as dependent upon the operation of some motivational complex.

In earlier work, three indexes of achievement-related motivation were constructed from attitudinal responses toward work which were elicited by the husband's questionnaire supplement to the initial interview.[11] These indexes

10 Blau and Duncan, *Occupational Structure*, pp. 374-88.
11 David L. Featherman, "The Socioeconomic Achievement of White Married Males in the United States: 1957-67." Ph.D. dissertation, University of Michigan, 1969, Chapter VII.

were originally constructed to provide estimates of socio-economic achievement (occupational prestige scores and dollars of salaries and wages) over the duration of the follow-up period (7-10 years); for the present discussion they can be characterized as measuring (to some degree) the desire or motivation to be mobile. One index, "Primary Work Orientation," attributed a positive valence to the work or job context. This positive value is non-economic in quality, but whether work was regarded as intrinsically satisfying as an activity or whether it was so regarded for its non-economic instrumental possibilities is not known. Agreement with the questionnaire items defining this construct indicated a preference for work rather than relaxation, a choice of the occupational work role over recreation. (Both the spending of time at an activity and the expressing of choice for it vis-à-vis some competing activity are behavioral indicators of motivational tendencies.)

A second index, "Materialistic Orientation," emphasized the material goals of the good life, goals achieved through work as instrumental activity. The items defining this second orientation suggested some expressed anxiety over the prospects of not attaining the desired level of material prosperity and incorporated a social comparative or reference group focus—material achievement which equals or surpasses that of neighbors and friends. The third index, "Subjective Achievement Evaluation," assessed the degree to which a man was satisfied with the educational, occupational, and economic achievements of his recent past; that is, the index serves as an indicator of the cumulative psychological effects of past and present socioeconomic achievements.

Data were drawn from couples interviewed at all three stages among whom the husband completed and returned the supplementary psychological questionnaire after the initial interview. These data include 715 of a possible 814 couples; characteristics of these cases with respect to the total sample are described elsewhere.[12] Suffice it to say that the data appear to be a reasonably reliable represen-

[12] *Ibid.*, Chapter IV.

tation of the original 1,165 cases, and regression analyses treating occupational and economic achievement for the whole set and the subset (at Panel I) produce quite similar estimates.

Table 43 records the coefficients of zero-order correlation between the three psychological indexes of achievement-related motivation and socioeconomic achievement as well as fertility, throughout the re-study period. If the disposition to be mobile is a determining condition of both the size of the family of procreation and the actual socioeconomic achievement, and if fertility and achievement are inversely related (as presumed by the mobility hypothesis), then the signs of the correlations between the psychological indexes and fertility and between the indexes and achievement should be opposite; that is, we would expect the psychological indices to be positively related to actual achievement but negatively related to fertility.

However, as observed in Table 43, although the disposition to be mobile can be employed to predict or estimate socioeconomic achievement,[13] the psychological indexes are

[13] We interpret the negative relationships between "Materialistic Orientation" and both the actual and subjectively perceived ("Subjective Achievement Evaluation") socioeconomic levels to indicate a dissatisfaction of high scorers on the index of materialistic orientation with their levels of education, occupation, and income achieved by the initial interview. However, responses of high materialistic orientation are observed both for Jews (whose average and perceived attainments are among the highest in the re-study period) and for Roman Catholics of (mainly) Italian and Mexican ancestry (whose actual and subjectively perceived achievements are the lowest). Thus, the index of materialistic orientation toward work can be interpreted as an indicator of achievement orientation, both for those whose social origins and educational achievements prevent comparatively high attainments in their socioeconomic careers (i.e., Roman Catholics) and for those who enjoy more beneficial socioeconomic backgrounds and educations with respect to occupation and income throughout the follow-up period (i.e., Jews). In our data, the Roman Catholics are approximately two and one-half times more numerous than the Jews; hence the negative correlation between materialistic orientation and socioeconomic achievements. When social origins, education, occupation, and income at the first interview are controlled statistically, the net regression coefficients for the effects of materialistic orientation on successive economic achievements are small but positive (Featherman, "Socioeconomic Achievement," Chapters VII and VIII).

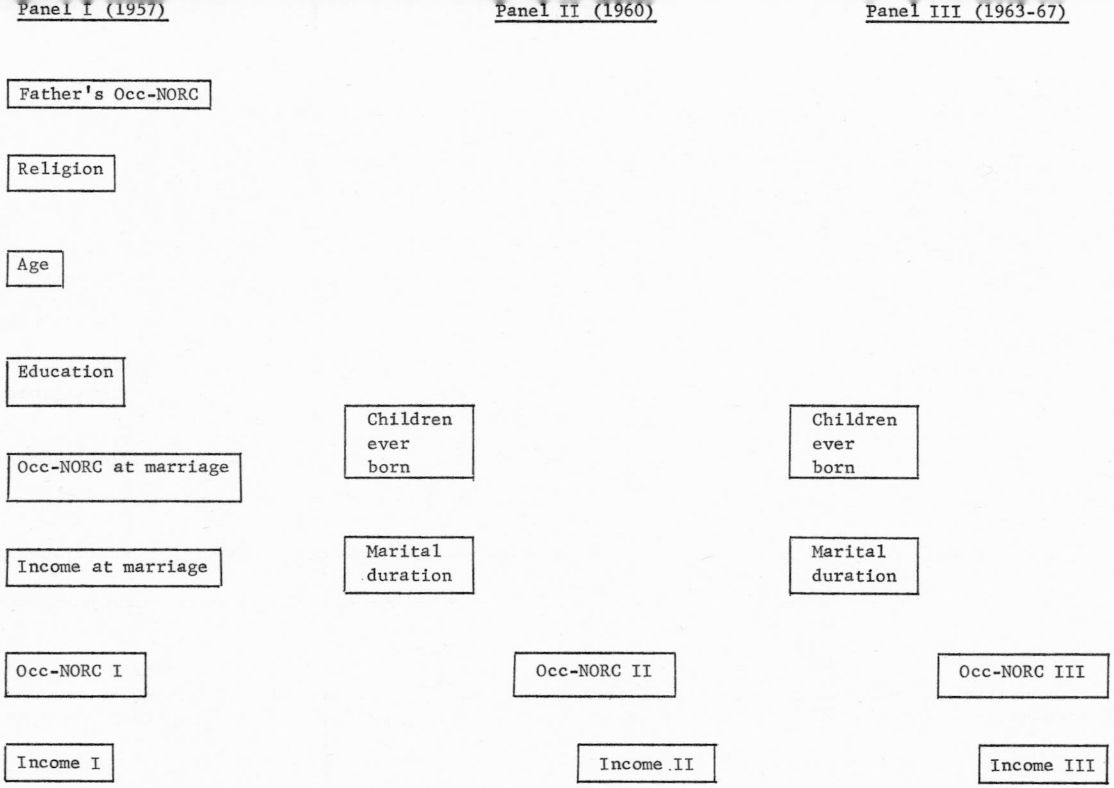

Figure 1. Conceptual model of cumulative fertility and marital duration as intervening variables in the process of socioeconomic achievement throughout the follow-up period of the Princeton Fertility Study

Table 43. Coefficients of correlation between three psychological indexes of achievement-related work motivations and socioeconomic and fertility variables throughout the follow-up period

Psychological indexes	Occ-NORC I	Income I	Occ-NORC II	Income II	Occ-NORC III	Income III	Live births I-II	Live births II-III	Live births I-III
Primary work orientation	.41	.24	.40	.28	.35	.31	.02	.02	.03
Materialistic orientation	-.12	-.06	-.09	-.05	-.11	-.01	-.01	-.01	-.01
Subjective achievement evaluation	.36	.33	.33	.40	.31	.34	.04	.04	.04

Source: This and all subsequent tables in this chapter are based on data for couples who were interviewed at all three panels and who completed and returned the husband's supplementary psychological questionnaire after the initial interview.

virtually uncorrelated with additional live births over the study period. Thus, the varieties of the weak mobility hypothesis which posit inverse relationships between the desire for upward mobility and family limitation are unsupported by our data.

Fertility and the Process of Achievement

It has yet to be examined whether high fertility impedes the process of socioeconomic achievement, or conversely, whether low fertility aids social mobility, as suggested by the mobility hypothesis. In this section we wish to assess the degree to which additional live births during the follow-up period were instrumental in influencing (positively or negatively) the levels of occupational and economic status, achieved by the husbands. This objective entails a restatement of the mobility hypothesis wherein marital fertility is regarded as an *intervening* variable between the occupational and economic statuses achieved by Panel I (1957) and those attained by the end of the re-study period (1963-67).

The present approach to the mobility hypothesis (weak form) places this idea in the context of the process of socioeconomic stratification, and as such it is only slightly different from the conceptualization of the issue by Duncan and his colleagues.[14] The analysis reported here is based on the conceptual model portrayed in Figure 1. Since socioeconomic achievement over the duration of the follow-up period is problematic in the ensuing discussion, the variables in the left column of Figure 1 are taken as predetermined. Thus, their intercorrelations are observed, and no assumptions of causation are advanced. Included in this first column of variables (all of which were reported at the initial interview) are the husband's occupational

[14] O. D. Duncan, David L. Featherman, and Beverly Duncan, "Socioeconomic Background and Occupational Achievement: Extensions of a Basic Model" (Final Report Project No. 5-0074 (EO-191), May 1968, The University of Michigan, Contract No. OE-5-85-072, Office of Education, Bureau of Research, Department of Health, Education, and Welfare), pp. 255-65.

status at marriage and at Panel I (coded into eleven five-point intervals on the 1947 NORC prestige scale),[15] his income at marriage and at Panel I (dollars of salary and wages),[16] years of schooling he completed, age (years), his father's longest occupation (1947 NORC interval), and his own religious preference (major religious faith).

Inclusion of paternal occupational status in the model permits us to assess the degree to which the socioeconomic status of the family of origin affects the socioeconomic career of the son, namely, to estimate the permeability[17] of the occupational structure for the subset of the American population covered in these data. Religious preference is treated here as another background variable, and it will be employed primarily as a classificatory variable. Age of the husband and age of the wife roughly denote the stages in the life cycle (point of development of the husband's career and the wife's childbearing years), and greater emphasis is placed on the age of the husband as a determinant of socioeconomic achievement throughout the re-study period (both for the whole data set and within categories formed by the age of his spouse). The importance of years of school completed as a direct force on levels of occupation and income achieved and as a major intervening variable between one's social origins and destinations has been well-documented elsewhere;[18] for the present discussion, the manner by which the father's social status and specific religious subgroup experiences affect occupational and economic achievements through differential years of education is left untreated. Previous research has shown the importance of prior occupational and economic statuses for the determination of successive career attainments. Moreover, statuses more remote in time from current

[15] National Opinion Research Center (NORC), "Jobs and Occupations: A Popular Evaluation," *Opinion News* 9 (1947): 3-13.

[16] Mid-points of statistical intervals of husband's salaries and wages were applied as individual scores.

[17] Kaare Svalastoga, *Social Differentiation* (New York: David McKay, 1965).

[18] Blau and Duncan, *Occupational Structure*.

achievements have direct bearing on present status, albeit the relationships are less forceful than for more proximate statuses.[19] This is to say that socioeconomic careers have a history or continuity, an aspect which is recognized by the inclusion of occupational and economic statuses at marriage and at Panel I as correlated measures of the early careers of the males in this study.

The major dependent variables under consideration are the occupational and income levels achieved at the second and third interviews. We do not employ a mobility variable (the difference between statuses at times one and two); rather, origin status and destination status are treated as separate components in the process denoted as social mobility. The merit of this procedure has been discussed fully by Duncan.[20]

Children ever born as determined in the second and third interviews comprise the independent variables of greatest importance in the present context. Occasionally we shall examine the influence of additional live births (during an interval between two panels) on socioeconomic achievements.[21] Finally, marriage duration is included as an independent variable in the model as a potential source of modification of the size of the family of procreation. As was true for the age variable, duration of marriage helps determine less ambiguously the direct effect of fertility on achievement for married men more or less at the same point in the life cycle.[22]

[19] Featherman, "Socioeconomic Achievement," Chapter VI.

[20] Blau and Duncan, *Occupational Structure*, pp. 194-99. The procedure becomes most obvious in regression analyses where the determinants of social mobility might operate differently with respect to the status of origin than with respect to that of destination. In any case, the decomposition entails no loss of information from that generated from the use of mobility variables.

[21] Since the data are for (originally) second-parity couples, variables such as children born between the first and second and the second and third interviews are equivalent to the variables of children ever born by Panel II and by Panel III.

[22] In these data, marriage duration recorded at the first interview is an indirect measure of fertility, since the duration of marriage to Panel I is (nearly) identical with the interval between marriage and the second birth.

Table 44. Means and standard deviations of selected variables

Variables	Means	Standard deviations
1. Father's Occ-NORC[a]	6.4	2.3
2. Education of husband (years)	12.9	2.7
3. Occ-NORC at marriage	6.6	2.2
4. Income at marriage (dollars)	5096.	2069.
5. Occ-NORC I	7.0	2.1
6. Income I	6407.	3829.
7. Occ-NORC II	7.1	2.3
8. Income II	8279.	4994.
9. Occ-NORC III	7.3	2.1
10. Income III	12881.	6602.
11. Fertility (live births) I-II	0.5	0.6
12. Fertility (live births)II-III[b]	0.5	0.5
13. Fertility (live births) I-III	1.2	1.2
14. Age (husband) I	29.6	4.6
15. Duration of marriage to II (years)	8.1	2.6
16. Duration of marriage to III	13.2	2.0
17. Interval (years) between II-III	5.2	1.5

[a] All Occ-NORC (1947) scores for occupational titles were aggregated into eleven five-unit intervals

[b] Dummy variable: 0 = no births; 1 = one or more births

114

Summary statistics are provided in Tables 44 and 45 and the generally upward mobility of the men in these data is apparent in Table 44. The trend toward vertical mobility can be observed in the increases in the respondents' mean occupational prestige scores both from the status of their families of origin and over the earlier occupational levels in their own careers since marriage. Featherman's[23] detailed description of the pattern and extent of father-son and career mobility in the data establishes that the majority of the upward movement between prestige score intervals consisted of relatively short distances. Correspondingly, the mean salaries and wages increased over the duration of the study period.

Table 46 provides a summary of the effects of socioeconomic background, educational achievements, and prior occupational and economic attainments on the successive levels of statuses achieved by the men between Panels I and III. These data describe the social structural context in which any potential intervening effects of fertility might function.[24]

The direct effect of social origins (father's occupation) on the socioeconomic career (net of other explanatory variables) is slightly greater in the earlier years of a man's labor force experience than in the middle years (or the end of the follow-up period), although the net effect of father's occupation seems to fall and then to rise between Panels I and III. Efforts to explain the "lagged effects" of

[23] Featherman, "Socioeconomic Achievement," Chapter V.

[24] Coefficients in Table 46 are partial regression coefficients for variables in standard form (means of unity and in units of their standard deviations), or *beta* coefficients. Values exceeding twice the absolute size of their standard errors are interpreted as stable estimates of the net effects of that variable on the dependent variables, after the effects of the other independent variables have been controlled statistically. Standardized variables allow us to interpret the sizes of the *beta* coefficients as indicating the relative importance of the explanatory variables, and all estimates of coefficients are a function of the specific set of variables in the regression equation. For a more detailed treatment of the substantive effects in Table 46 see Featherman, "Socioeconomic Achievement," Chapter VI.

115

Table 45. Coefficients of correlation for background, socioeconomic status, and family-building variables

Variables	X_1	X_2	X_3	X_4	X_5	X_6	X_7	X_8	X_9	X_{10}	X_{11}	X_{12}	X_{13}	X_{14}	X_{15}	X_{16}	X_{17}
Father's Occ-NORC (X_1)	--	.34	.29	.10	.33	.15	.30	.20	.34	.24	.00	-.06	-.05	-.03	-.05	-.07	-.00
Education (husband) (X_2)			.60	.14	.64	.32	.65	.44	.60	.48	-.01	-.02	-.04	.13	-.01	-.08	-.10
Occ-NORC at mar. (X_3)				.22	.73	.37	.64	.44	.58	.42	-.02	-.07	-.05	.14	.01	-.08	-.14
Income at mar. (X_4)					.11	.34	.08	.24	.09	.20	.06	-.01	.01	.17	-.15	-.26	-.08
Occ-NORC I (X_5)						.34	.78	.44	.69	.47	-.02	-.06	-.06	.12	.03	-.02	-.09
Income I (X_6)							.32	.62	.27	.40	-.06	-.09	-.12	.17	.10	.05	-.10
Occ-NORC II (X_7)								.44	.74	.47	.01	-.03	-.03	.09	.02	-.05	-.10
Income II (X_8)									.40	.52	-.03	-.06	-.07	.15	.04	-.04	-.11
Occ-NORC III (X_9)										.51	.05	.02	.04	.00	-.06	-.08	-.02
Income III (X_{10})											.04	-.02	.01	-.02	-.08	-.04	.09
Fert. (live births) I-II (X_{11})												.18	.71	-.24	-.33	-.24	.26
Fert. (live births) II-III* (X_{12})													.70	-.32	-.38	-.23	.37
Fert. (live births) I-III (X_{13})														-.35	-.46	-.29	.42
Age (husband) I (X_{14})															.62	.31	-.67
Duration of marriage to II (X_{15})																.82	-.64
Duration of marriage to III (X_{16})																	-.10
Interval (years) II-III (X_{17})																	--

* dummy variable

Table 46. Partial regression coefficients (in standard form) for occupational and economic achievement at four points in the life cycle on background and previous statuses

Independent variables	Dependent variables							
	X_3	X_4	X_5	X_6	X_7	X_8	X_9	X_{10}
Father's Occ-NORC (X_1)	.10	.03[a]	.08	.00[a]	.01[a]	.01[a]	.08	.02[a]
Education (X_2)	.56	.01[a]	.29	.12	.24	.13	.12	.13
Occ-NORC at mar. (X_3)	---	.20	.54	.14	.10	.07[a]	.04[a]	-.02[a]
Income at mar. (X_4)		---	-.06	.28	-.05	.02[a]	-.00[a]	.05[a]
Occ-NORC I (X_5)			---	.13	.54	.05[a]	.20	.06[a]
Income I (X_6)				---	.03[a]	.49	-.03[a]	.09
Occ-NORC II (X_7)					---	.12	.44	.00[a]
Income II (X_8)						---	.04[a]	.27
Occ-NORC III (X_9)							---	.26
Income III (X_{10})								---
Coefficient of determination	.36	.05	.60	.23	.65	.48	.60	.41

[a] Coefficient less than twice its standard error.

paternal occupational status in the middle of the filial occupational career in terms of either increased "occupational inheritance" or the operation of achievement-related motivations and values that were learned in the family of socialization fail to account for this positive net effect on occupation at Panel III.[25] Consistent with the findings of Blau and Duncan, our data demonstrate that the major expression for the effects of social origins is an indirect one, through the years of schooling which the economic, social, and psychological resources of the family of orientation could provide for the son. The son's education more strongly influences occupational achievements in the initial stages of the career, and the net, direct effects of years of schooling completed decline over the follow-up period. In contrast, the net effects of education on income rise between Panels I and III. For men with equal occupations of origin and destination, those with more education earn larger incomes; but the income differentials per year of schooling are greater at the end of the re-study period than at the initial interview. Thus men initiating their occupational careers are handicapped economically by their lack of tenure and labor force experience.

The effects of prior socioeconomic attainments accumulate over the course of the career. For example, the occupational status at marriage not only affects the occupational status at Panel I, but it also has a statistically significant net effect on the occupational prestige score at Panel II (an effect greater than that of the other independent variables, including occupation at Panel I). These data suggest that the socioeconomic career entails a history which cannot be accurately approximated by models of occupational achievement like simple causal chains or Markovian processes.[26]

It is in this context of socioeconomic achievement that we now examine the role of the fertility and life-cycle varia-

[25] *Ibid.*, Chapter VII.
[26] *Ibid.*, Chapter VI; see also Robert W. Hodge, "Occupational Mobility as a Probability Process," *Demography* 3 (1966): 19-34.

bles. In the structural equations for the determination of occupation and income at Panel II (Table 47), the coefficients for social background, education, and prior achieved status effects are barely affected by the introduction of the fertility and life-cycle variables, and the *beta* coefficients for the latter variables fail the criterion of statistical significance. These latter independent variables neither add new sources of explained variance to the social structural model of socioeconomic achievement (Table 46) nor function as intervening variables (capable of explaining how social background or education influence later achieved statuses), as seen in the corresponding coefficients of multiple determination in Tables 46 and 47.

For the socioeconomic statuses at the terminal interview (Table 48), cumulative fertility does contribute a small positive influence on occupation, after the effects of social background, education, and prior achieved statuses are controlled statistically. Under the imputed causal assumptions in Figure 1, additional children in the follow-up period induce higher levels of occupational achievement for men who have equivalent social origins, educations, prior socioeconomic levels, and who are at nearly the same point in the life-cycle (indexed by age and duration of marriage). In terms of the variance explained by these structural equations, cumulative fertility adds 0.6 percent to that explained by the background and achievement variables alone, and in conjunction with the other life-cycle variables this increment rises to 0.9 percent.

In Table 48 and elsewhere we hesitate to place great emphasis on the gross and net relationships between the fertility (and life-cycle) variables and economic achievement at Panel III. The study design permitted a variable number of years in the re-study period for couples selected on criteria such as age, duration of marriage, and family-size desires. In particular, the number of years between the second and third panels varied between 3 and 7. Previous analysis of the potential effects of this aspect of the design for the study of socioeconomic achievement has shown that

119

Table 47. Partial regression coefficients (in standard form) relating background, achieved status, and family-building variables to socioeconomic achievement at Panel II

Independent variables	Socioeconomic achievement at Panel II							
	Occ-NORC II				Income II			
Father's (husband's) Occ-NORC	$.01^a$	$.01^a$	$.01^a$	$.01^a$	$.02^a$	$.02^a$	$.01^a$	$.02^a$
Education (husband)	.24	.24	.24	.24	.15	.15	.12	.12
Occ-NORC at marriage	.11	.11	.11	.11	$.08^a$	$.08^a$	$.07^a$	$.07^a$
Income at marriage	-.05	-.05	-.05	$-.05^a$	$.02^a$	$.02^a$	$.02^a$	$.01^a$
Occ-NORC I	.54	.54	.54	.54	.11	.11	$.05^a$	$.05^a$
Income I	$.04^a$	$.04^a$	$.04^a$	$.04^a$	.50	.49	.49	.49
Occ-NORC II	...	...	...	...	...	...	.12	.12
Income II	...	...	...	...	...	...	...	...
Fertility (live births) I-II	$.03^a$	$.03^a$	$.03^a$	$.03^a$	$.00^a$	$.00^a$	$-.01^a$	$-.00^a$
Age (husband) II	$-.01^a$	...	...	$-.02^a$	...	$.02^a$	...	$.05^a$
Duration of marriage to II	...	...	$.00^a$	$.01^a$	...	...	$-.01^a$	$-.04^a$
Coefficient of determination	.65	.65	.65	.65	.47	.47	.48	.48

^{a} Coefficient less than twice its standard error.

Table 48. Partial regression coefficients (in standard form) relating background, achieved status, and family-building variables to socioeconomic achievement at Panel III

Independent variables	Socioeconomic achievement at Panel III							
	Occ-NORC III				Income III			
Father's Occ-NORC	.09	.08	.09	.08	.01[a]	.01[a]	-.00[a]	-.00[a]
Education	.12	.12	.12	.12	.15	.14	.16	.15
Occ-NORC at marriage	.05[a]	.05[a]	.04[a]	.05[a]	-.02[a]	-.02[a]	-.01[a]	-.00[a]
Income at marriage	-.01[a]	.00[a]	-.01[a]	.00[a]	.07	.06[a]	.09	.08
Occ-NORC I	.20	.21	.21	.21	.07[a]	.06[a]	.06[a]	.05[a]
Income I	-.02[a]	-.02[a]	-.02[a]	-.02[a]	.10	.09	.09	.09
Occ-NORC II	.44	.43	.43	.43	.01[a]	.00[a]	.01[a]	.02[a]
Income II	.04[a]	.05[a]	.04[a]	.05[a]	.27	.27	.27	.28
Occ-NORC III	...	...	...	...	.24	.27	.26	.26
Fertility (live births) I-III	.08	.05	.07	.05	-.01[a]	.04[a]	.00[a]	-.04[a]
Age (husband) I	...	-.07	...	-.07	-.12	...	-.14	-.04[a]
Duration marriage to III	...	...	-.02[a]	.00[a]	...	.03[a]	.07	.04[a]
Interval II-III	...	...	...	...	...	...	...	.16
Coefficient of determination	.60	.61	.60	.61	.42	.42	.43	.44

[a] Coefficient less than twice its standard error

they are not identifiably critical for occupational statuses at the terminal interview, but the variable number of years does affect the variation in income.[27] Such an influence is visible in the last column of Table 48, where the net effect of the temporal interval between Panels II and III is positive and statistically significant. However, in none of the structural equations is the net effect of cumulative fertility statistically greater than zero.

Table 49 decomposes the cumulative fertility for the follow-up period into the number of live births between Panels I and II and between Panels II and III. The latter variable was coded into two categories (0 for no additional births; 1 for one or more) on the reasoning that all women had sufficient time to bear at least one child in the interval II-III, but that the unequal number of years between the second and third interviews might affect the variation more markedly in a variable coded in single birth units. Data for the two fertility variables indicate that the net effect of additional births in each between-panel interval on occupational achievement at the terminal interview is quite small and positive. Prior to adjustment of the data for variation in age and duration of marriage, both *beta* coefficients for inter-panel fertility are of nearly equal size, but only the coefficient for the period II-III is acceptably larger than its standard error. Although both fertility values remain of similar magnitude to each other after the life-cycle variables (specifically age) are introduced, neither absolute value is sufficiently greater than its standard error.

Again, the interpretation of the *beta* coefficients for the effects of inter-panel fertility on income at Panel III is beclouded by the study design. The signs on the coefficients, all but one of which is non-significant, would indicate that the net effect of fertility between Panels I and II is positive, while between II and III it is negative; this is the pattern of the gross relationships as well (.04 and —.02, respectively,

[27] Featherman, "Socioeconomic Achievement," Chapter IV.

Table 49. Partial regression coefficients (in standard form) relating background, achieved status, and family-building variables to socioeconomic achievement at Panel III: an expansion

Independent variables	Socioeconomic achievement at Panel III					
	Occ-NORC III			Income III		
Father's Occ-NORC	.09	.08	.08	.01[a]	-.00[a]	-.00[a]
Education	.12	.12	.12	.14	.16	.15
Occ-NORC marriage	.05[a]	.05[a]	.05[a]	-.02[a]	-.02[a]	-.00[a]
Income marriage	-.01[a]	.00[a]	.00[a]	.05[a]	.09	.08
Occ-NORC I	.20	.21	.21	.06[a]	.06[a]	.04[a]
Income I	-.02[a]	-.02[a]	-.02[a]	.10	.09	.09
Occ-NORC II	.43	.43	.43	-.00[a]	.01[a]	.02[a]
Income II	.04[a]	.05[a]	.05[a]	.26	.27	.28
Occ-NORC III	...	...	...	.26	.27	.26
Income III	...	...	...	...	...	...
Fertility (live births) I-II	.04[a]	.03[a]	.03[a]	.04[a]	.02[a]	.01[a]
Fertility (live births) II-III (dummy)	.05	.03[a]	.03[a]	-.00[a]	-.03[a]	-.06
Age (husband) I	...	-.07	-.07	...	-.15	-.04[a]
Duration marriage to III	...	.00[a]	-.00[a]	...	.07	.04[a]
Interval II-III	...	...	.00[a]	...	...	.16
Coefficient of determination	.60	.61	.61	.42	.43	.45

[a] Coefficient less than twice its standard error.

in Table 45). When the respondents' social background, prior achieved statuses, and stage in the life-cycle are equalized, the negative net effect of the Panel II-III fertility on salaries and wages at the terminal interview increases, while the positive net effect of Panel I-II fertility (non-significant) decreases. These small changes in the equally small coefficients (under controls for stage in the life-cycle), however, are not interpreted substantively, since they undoubtedly reflect some selection of couples for differential II-III intervals by life-cycle characteristics at Panel II. In the final column of Table 49, the introduction of the variable indicating the length of the interval between the second and third interviews enlarges the negative value of the *beta* coefficient for the dummy fertility variable (II-III). This significantly negative coefficient would suggest that the net effect of additional births later in the follow-up period serves to depress the level of income (slightly) for men of equal origin and destination occupations, educations, and stages in the life-cycle. We view this net effect with great caution, however, given its magnitude and the rather uncertain effects of the study design on the relationship between fertility and economic achievement at the end of the follow-up period.

In summary of Tables 47-49 we find the net effects of cumulative fertility (and/or additional live births) on both occupational and economic achievement throughout the follow-up period to be virtually non-existent. The signs on the net effects are essentially positive for occupational achievement and negative for economic achievement, *whenever these net coefficients are larger than twice their standard errors.* Gross relationships between the inter-panel fertility variables and Panel III socioeconomic status variables (Table 45) are extremely small, but the signs are consistent with the net effects ($r_{11,7} = .01$, $r_{11,8} = -.03$; $r_{12,9} = .02$, $r_{12,10} = -.02$). Were the data not restricted to a population of second-parity couples, the variation in the fertility variables would presumably be somewhat greater as would the covariation between fertility and socioeconomic variables. Thus, these data ought not be used as estimates of the gross and net relationships between fertility and achievement in a more general population.[28]

From these data, we find little support for the line of reasoning that advances a net causal relationship between family size (antecedent) and socioeconomic achievement (consequence). Of course, the process whereby cumulative fertility influences the course of the socioeconomic career might not be approximated by linear models, or it could operate differentially (in such a manner as to produce a nearly zero correlation) for selected subgroups. On the latter possibility, we examined the relationship between fertility and achievement within categories of the wife's age. However, the data in Table 50 indicate a close correspondence between the subgroups with respect to the absence of a significant effect of cumulative fertility on occupation and income at Panel III.

Religious Subgroups

Research in this and other fertility studies has documented variation in fertility by religious preference subgroups. For example, we see in Table 51 (column 1) that nearly one child separates the Jewish husbands from the Roman Catholic husbands with respect to the number of live births to their wives during the follow-up period. Religious differentials in fertility have been treated elsewhere in this volume, but we note that when the religious subgroups are equated statistically for their social origins, education, and socioeconomic achievements to Panel I (column 2 of Table 51), the variation in subgroup fertility is not reduced. This, of course, is another way of saying that these social structural variables in the linear regression model provide rather poor estimates of the fertility of religious subgroups in these data.

Our interest here, however, is in the potential effect of

[28] Persons interested in such estimates might consult Duncan, Featherman, and Duncan, "Socioeconomic Background," Tables 9.5.1. and 9.5.2.

Table 50. Partial regression coefficients for background, achieved statuses, and fertility effects on occupational and economic achievement at Panel III, by age of wife at Panel I

	Age of wife (years) at Panel I											
	<25.0 (N=266)				25.0-29.9 (N=277)				≥30.0 (N=172)			
Independent variables	Occ-NORC III	Occ-NORC III	Income III	Income III	Occ-NORC III	Occ-NORC III	Income III	Income III	Occ-NORC III	Occ-NORC III	Income III	Income III
Father's Occ-NORC	.14	.15	86.2[a]	42.7[a]	.04[a]	.04[a]	140.3[a]	141.6[a]	.03[a]	.01[a]	-255.5[a]	-280.1[a]
Education	.18	.18	434.1	417.4	.07	.07	530.8	523.7	.03[a]	.04[a]	103.7[a]	125.4[a]
Occ-NORC at mar.	.02[a]	.02[a]	172.1[a]	168.9[a]	.11	.11	-341.0[a]	-339.1[a]	-.07[a]	-.06[a]	247.7[a]	217.8[a]
Income at mar.	-.00[a]	-.00[a]	0.6	0.6	-.00[a]	-.00[a]	0.1[a]	0.1[a]	.00[a]	.00[a]	0.1[a]	0.1[a]
Occ-NORC I	.19	.19	92.9[a]	124.0[a]	.14	.14	158.6[a]	137.8[a]	.36	.35	354.7[a]	344.1[a]
Income I	-.00[a]	-.00[a]	0.0[a]	0.0[a]	-.00[a]	-.00[a]	0.3	0.2	.00[a]	.00[a]	0.1[a]	0.1[a]
Occ-NORC II	.39	.39	185.2[a]	174.0[a]	.44	.44	-96.3[a]	-49.9[a]	.57	.56	10.9[a]	31.9[a]
Income II	.00[a]	.00[a]	0.2	0.2	.00[a]	.00[a]	0.3	0.3	-.00[a]	-.00[a]	0.6	0.6
Occ-NORC III	---	---	753.4	794.5	---	---	1079.8	1048.9	---	---	534.7	559.9[a]
Fertility I - III	.11[a]	.11[a]	-209.0[a]	-213.6[a]	.08[a]	.11[a]	-114.2[a]	-278.1[a]	.09[a]	.03[a]	-139.2[a]	-68.4[a]
Age (husband)	---	-.00[a]	---	-125.0[a]	---	-.04[a]	---	-94.3[a]	---	-.05[a]	---	13.5[a]
Interval II - III	---	-.33[a]	---	1429.4[a]	---	.05[a]	---	459.3[a]	---	.08[a]	---	-924.8[a]
Coefficient of determination	.50	.51	.36	.38	.66	.66	.50	.50	.71	.72	.54	.54

[a] Coefficient less than twice its standard error.

Table 51. Gross and net effects of religious preference, background and achieved statuses, and cumulative fertility

Independent variables	Fertility (live births) I - III		Occ-NORC III				Income III			
						Dependent variables				
Religion										
Jewish	-.62[a]	-.64[b]	.85[a]	.98[b]	-.05[b]	.06[b]	2986.[a]	3241.[b]	581.[b]	728.[b]
Protestant	-.23	-.23	.20	.24	-.03	.01	370.	464.	-121.	-69.
Roman Catholics	.38	.37	-.45	-.53	-.01	-.08	-1107.	-1259.	17.	-70.
None; Other	.01	.00	.39	.39	.45	.45	-346.	-349.	-631.	-623.
Background and achieved statuses										
Father's Occ-NORC	--	-.00	--	--	.06	.07	--	--	91.	93.
Education	--	.03	--	--	.17	.17	--	--	401.	397.
Occ-NORC at mar.	--	-.00	--	--	.09	.09	--	--	-3.	-1.
Income at mar.	--	.00	--	--	-.00	-.00	--	--	0.	0.
Occ-NORC I	--	.01	--	--	.46	.46	--	--	213.	220.
Income I	--	-.00	--	--	.00	.00	--	--	0.	0.
Occ-NORC III	--	--	--	--	--	--	--	--	966.	231.
Fertility between I-III	--	--	--	.20	--	.16	--	407.	--	947.

[a] Gross deviations about the grand mean; gross effects
[b] Partial regression (metric) coefficients; net effects

religious subgroup fertility on the variation in the socio-economic achievement of Jews, Roman Catholics, and Protestants. Data in Table 51 reveal that an approximately 0.6 standard deviation separates the occupational and economic achievements (gross deviations about the grand means at Panel III) of the Jewish men from those of the Roman Catholics. Intermediate between the over-achieving Jews and the under-achieving Catholics is the socioeconomic performance of the Protestants. If we treat the religious subgroups as dummy variables in a regression equation, then adjusting the subgroup variation in occupation and income at Panel III for differential fertility during the follow-up period has little effect on the coefficients for subgroup achievement. Such an adjustment only slightly widens the gap between the achievement of Jewish and Catholic males, owing to the positive net effect of fertility on occupation and income and to the fewer children sired by Jewish fathers, when compared to their Catholic counterparts.

A substantial reduction in the religious subgroup socioeconomic differentials occurs when the effects of social origins, education, and prior occupational and economic attainments are controlled statistically. Elsewhere it has been demonstrated that such a procedure effectively reduces religious (and ethnic) variation in socioeconomic achievement at Panel III to zero.[29] Thus, virtually all religious achievement differentials at Panel III can be attributed to the relative advantages and disadvantages of social background, education, and early career attainments. Adding differential fertility during the follow-up period to these sources of subgroup socioeconomic attainments (column 6 and 10) produces only slight changes in the partial regression coefficients, indicating that the role of fertility as an intervening variable between the effects of social background, religious subgroup background, or past

[29] Featherman, "Socioeconomic Achievement," Chapter VIII.

achieved statuses and socioeconomic achievements at Panel III is a doubtful one.

To complete our assessment of the relationship between fertility and socioeconomic achievement for religious subgroups, we examined some linear models of achievement within each of the three major religious subgroups (Table 52). Concentrating on the partial regression (unstandardized or metric) coefficients for the fertility effects, we find differences in the magnitudes of the values, but little persuasive evidence of a significant interaction between fertility and socioeconomic achievement. Thus, for religious subgroups as for the entire sample, there appears to be little relationship between differential fertility and socioeconomic achievement.

Summary and Conclusions

While we find no support in these data for the mobility hypothesis (as presently stated), the data provide only a limited test of the predicted relationship between fertility and mobility. We have studied second-parity couples and their subsequent fertility (a mean of 1.2 additional births during the follow-up period and a variance of about 1.5). Had the data been drawn from a more representative cross-section of the population, we would expect the variation in fertility to be greater and the estimates of the fertility-achievement relationships to be on the order of those reported by Duncan et al.[30] Additionally, the metropolitan character of our data undoubtedly fails to represent the degree of movement from farm to nonfarm occupations which obtains in the general population. Blau and Duncan note that such mobility constitutes an important source of the relationship between fertility and mobility.[31] However, as the extent of farm to nonfarm mobility declines, Blau and Duncan suggest that the traditional mobility hypothesis grows more irrelevant; our data concur with their conjec-

[30] Duncan, Featherman, and Duncan, "Socioeconomic Background."
[31] Blau and Duncan, *Occupational Structure*, p. 390.

Table 52. Partial regression coefficients for background, achieved statuses, and fertility effects on occupational and economic achievement at Panel III, by husband's religious preference subgroups

Independent variables	Protestant (N=273)				Roman Catholic (N=317)				Jewish (N=88)				Total[b] (N=715)			
	Occ-NORC III		Income III		Occ-NORC III		Income III		Occ-NORC III		Income III		Occ-NORC III		Income III	
Father's Occ-NORC	.11	.09	22.1[a]	-3.3[a]	.06[a]	.06[a]	16.1[a]	-16.9[a]	.03[a]	-.00[a]	337.5[a]	306.7[a]	.08	.07	27.5[a]	19.8[a]
Education	.10	.10	208.5[a]	201.5[a]	.07[a]	.07[a]	485.9	504.7	.09[a]	.09[a]	101.2[a]	280.9[a]	.09	.10	336.7	355.2
Occ-NORC at mar.	-.01[a]	.01[a]	-363.6[a]	-314.3[a]	.11	.10[a]	220.2[a]	291.8[a]	-.09[a]	-.10[a]	-265.4[a]	-288.3[a]	-.04[a]	-.05[a]	-75.7[a]	-1.2[a]
Income at mar.	-.00[a]	.00[a]	0.2[a]	0.3[a]	.00[a]	.00[a]	-0.0[a]	0.0[a]	-.00[a]	-.00[a]	0.1[a]	0.2[a]	-.00[a]	.00[a]	0.2	0.2
Occ-NORC I	.18	.19	622.8	667.0	.20	.20	43.7[a]	-108.8[a]	.36	.39	-661.1[a]	-565.5[a]	.20	.21	180.7[a]	158.8[a]
Income I	-.00[a]	-.00[a]	0.1[a]	0.1[a]	-.00[a]	.00[a]	0.3	0.4	-.00[a]	-.00[a]	0.2[a]	0.1[a]	-.00[a]	-.00[a]	0.2	0.2
Occ-NORC II	.51	.51	-206.4[a]	-143.6[a]	.43	.43	-38.8[a]	48.2[a]	.46	.41	535.3[a]	384.9[a]	.45	.45	4.3[a]	67.8[a]
Income II	.00[a]	.00[a]	0.4	0.4	-.00[a]	-.00[a]	0.4	0.4	.00[a]	.00[a]	0.3	0.3	-.00[a]	-.00[a]	0.3	0.4
Occ-NORC III	---	---	1024.2	930.6	---	---	614.5	654.9	---	---	1284.4	1122.9[a]	---	---	858.9	762.2
Fertility I - III	.22	.10[a]	239.7[a]	-142.2[a]	.12	.13[a]	258.5[a]	-224.4[a]	.10[a]	-.00[a]	499.7[a]	212.8[a]	.13	.09	172.6[a]	-238.7[a]
Age (husband)	---	-.03[a]	---	-89.7[a]	---	-.03[a]	---	81.2[a]	---	.03[a]	---	-246.8[a]	---	-.03[a]	---	-27.1[a]
Interval II - III	---	.09[a]	---	345.4[a]	---	-.09[a]	---	1307.2	---	.10[a]	---	-270.5[a]	---	-.00[a]	---	792.3
Coefficient of determination	.64	.65	.42	.43	.54	.54	.40	.46	.77	.79	.45	.47	.60	.61	.42	.44

[a] Coefficient less than twice its standard error.

[b] Total includes others and nonrespondents on religion.

ture. In any case, the data pertain to a rather specialized subset of the American population and comprise a sample of neither a distinct set of birth cohorts nor a set of marriage cohorts. As such, they are less than ideal to speak to the issue of fertility and socioeconomic achievement in the general population.

For a subset of the white metropolitan population, however, there is no compelling evidence for any strong relationship between fertility and socioeconomic achievement and no support for the varieties of the mobility hypothesis which were considered above. We find a small *positive* net effect of fertility during the re-study period on the occupational and economic achievements at the termination of the study, after all men are equated statistically for social origins, past educational and socioeconomic achievements, and their points in the life-cycle. Moreover, there is little indication that the near zero correlations between the fertility variables and the socioeconomic attainments are a function of non-linear or compensating relationships between religious subgroups or categories based on the age of the wife.

131

VIII · The Reliability of Retrospective Reporting on Fertility and Fertility Control

The study of fertility has become increasingly dependent upon the use of survey data. By interviewing a cross-sectional sample of the population it is possible to collect detailed information on fertility and fertility planning not otherwise obtainable. Since retrospective reports of contraceptive behavior and attitudes prior to each conception are vital to the understanding of the dynamics of fertility control, it is important to evaluate the reliability of such reports.

When a 35-year-old woman is interviewed about the circumstances preceding her first pregnancy, she is being asked to report events (and often her feelings about those events) which occurred more than 10 years earlier. How reliable are such data? Most studies, because they are one-time surveys, are at best able to evaluate the internal consistency of their data. A considerable advance in the evaluation of reliability was made in the 1965 National Fertility Study through the technique of follow-up interviews with a subsample of the women originally interviewed 3 to 4 months earlier.[1] While yielding much useful information, such a re-survey provides maximal estimates of reliability since only a brief period of time separates the two reports as compared with the time intervals that typically elapse between fertility events and the reports on those events collected in cross-sectional surveys.

The data described here offer a rather unique opportunity to compare the respondent's report 6 months after the second birth about events preceding that birth with her report of the same events collected 6 to 10 years later. A

[1] Ryder and Westoff, *Reproduction in the United States: 1965*, Appendix A.

132

similar analysis of these data was conducted based on a 3-year interval.[2]

Although other comparisons are possible, attention will be focused here on the consistency with which events preceding the second birth were reported at the first and third interviews.

Pregnancy Histories

As described in Chapter I, the Princeton Study was initially restricted to women with very simple pregnancy histories: all had borne two children and none had experienced more than one miscarriage. Nevertheless, among women who reported a miscarriage before the first interview, at the second interview 3 years later only 23 percent reported that miscarriage consistently with respect to pregnancy order and month of occurrence. For 47 percent, the date of miscarriage was inconsistently reported, and for the remaining 30 percent this miscarriage was not even mentioned at the second interview.[3] Miscarriages are much less salient to most women than live births, and consequently they often recall the experience inaccurately, if at all.

The extreme unreliability of reports on dates of miscarriages poses a serious problem for their use in analyses of pregnancy timing patterns; but inconsistent reporting of the fact that a miscarriage has occurred creates more general problems. Over 30 percent of all women experience at least one miscarriage some time in their married life. The unreliability of the recall of these events could contribute materially to the study of differential fertility when the number of conceptions is the measure employed. Further problems arise in longitudinal studies. Whenever a miscarriage is reported at one interview but not at another, the same pregnancy—for example the pregnancy preceding the second birth—is reported as a different preg-

---

[2] Westoff, Potter, and Sagi, *The Third Child*, Appendix C.
[3] *Ibid.*, p. 265.

nancy order in the two interviews. In extreme cases the same event may be reported as a different pregnancy order at each of the three interviews. If a woman reports single miscarriages of different orders at different interviews, it is impossible to determine whether the same event is being reported incorrectly with respect to pregnancy order or whether different events are being alternately reported and forgotten.

A woman's fertility history is classified as involving a major discrepancy if a miscarriage of a given order is reported at the first or second interview but not at a subsequent interview or if a miscarriage is reported at the second or third interview which should have been reported at an earlier interview. When pregnancy histories reported at the three interviews are compared, a major discrepancy exists in 28 percent of the cases reporting a miscarriage, or 8 percent of all cases (Table 53). This high unreliability of miscarriage data and its implications for the measurement of fertility suggests that the most judicious approach may be to concentrate primarily on effective fertility, that is preg-

Table 53. Major inconsistencies in pregnancy histories

Type of pregnancy history and discrepancy	Number	Percent
Total	814	100.0
History does not include miscarriage	570	70.0
History includes miscarriage:		
No major discrepancy	176	21.6
Major discrepancy	68	8.4

nancies terminating in live births. This is the procedure followed in this volume.

Use of Contraception and Methods Used

While there was aggregate stability between the first and third interviews in the proportion reporting use of contraception in the second birth interval, this stability results from counterbalancing discrepancies on the part of 17 percent of the sample (Table 54). Apparently, recall of the use of contraception after 6 to 10 years is no worse than recall after 3 years. The fact that there is aggregate stability independent of the length of the recall time is reassuring to attempts to estimate trends in contraceptive use based on retrospective data. On the other hand, individual discrepancies may have serious consequences for the study of patterns among women who do or do not use contraception.

The population of "users" as reported at the third interview is for the most part the same as that reported at the first interview. Analyses based on "users" as reported 6 to 10 years after the event may erroneously include about 10 percent who were not in fact users at the time of the event in question. An error of this magnitude would downwardly bias estimates of contraceptive efficacy among users and would also bias estimates of relationships between contraceptive efficacy and whatever variables might be associated with reliability, but the problems introduced by a classification error of this magnitude do not seem particularly serious.

Analyses of "non-users" of contraception risk much more serious biases. Of those who reported at the third interview that they did not use contraception in the second birth interval, two-fifths had reported such use at the first interview. Estimates of conception time for women not using contraception would be considerably inflated if based on data in which over two-fifths of the population classified as "non-users" had in fact used contraception. This may be

135

Table 54. Reliability in reporting use and non-use of contraception
for second birth interval

	Number	Percent
Comparison between first and third interviews		
Total	814	100.0
Use of contraception reported in both interviews	586	72.0
Use reported in first interview, non-use in third	69	8.5
Non-use reported in first interview, use in third	67	8.2
Non-use reported in both interviews	92	11.3
Comparison between first and second interviews[a]		
Total	863	100.0
Use of contraception reported in both interviews	628	72.8
Use reported in first interview, non-use in second	67	7.8
Non-use reported in first interview, use in second	63	7.3
Non-use reported in both interviews	105	12.2

[a]Westoff, Potter, and Sagi, The Third Child, Table C-2

one reason why conception waits are often found to be
longer for non-users than for users of contraception.[4] The
size of this bias makes questionable the practice of conduct-
ing separate analyses for non-users of contraception.

[4] Ibid., pp. 33-36; Westoff, Potter, Sagi, and Mishler, Family
Growth, pp. 57-66.

Consistency of Methods Reported

Turning to the type of contraceptive method reported, we again find that high aggregate stability results from many counterbalancing discrepancies. The comparison of reports of methods used is complicated by the fact that two or more methods may be reported at one interview and only one of those methods reported at another. While such reports are not wholly consistent, they are more so than are reports in which there is no overlap. Table 55 summarizes the comparisons between the first and third interview reports by type of method reported at the first interview. The third interview report is identical with the first for only about half the women, although for an additional 27 percent at least one method is common to the two reports.

Reliability varies markedly with the type of method reported. Use of either the condom or the diaphragm with jelly is recalled quite accurately over this 8-year interval. Of those reporting these methods at the first interview, less than 20 percent give completely inconsistent third interview reports. Rhythm is only somewhat less reliably reported, whereas withdrawal and douche are least likely to be reported consistently. Over two-thirds of the women reporting douche and over one-half of those reporting withdrawal at the first interview fail to report these methods at the third interview. When multiple methods are reported, the exact combination is seldom recalled although at least one of the multiple methods is usually reported at the third interview. Combinations involving rhythm are not particularly less reliably recalled than other combinations. In fact, rhythm is no more likely to be "forgotten" when originally reported in conjunction with other methods than when originally reported as the sole method used. It is particularly interesting that those methods involving the least artificial interference—withdrawal, douche, and rhythm—are the very ones most often confused with "no method."

We noted above that recall of the use of contraception

137

is as good over a 6- to 10-year period as it is over a 3-year period. This is not true of recall of the method used. For each method type reported at the first interview, the proportion reporting the same method is lower at the third than at the second interview.

The data in Table 55 have several implications for the use of retrospective survey data on contraceptive methods. The fact that the most effective methods are reported most reliably implies that women who are erroneously classified as "non-users" are disproportionately likely to have used the more ineffective methods.[5] More importantly, it is difficult to isolate populations using specific methods. Since women who reported multiple methods at the first interview were most likely to report only one of those methods at the third interview, women classified some 8 years after the event as having used a single method include many who used that method in combination with other methods. Attempts to make comparisons among the various methods with respect to acceptability or efficacy would have a relatively high level of disturbance from this source, *even if* use of the given method were reliably reported. At the third interview 480 cases reported use of a single method in the second birth interval; of these, 27 percent had not reported this method at the first interview (immediately after the second birth) and an additional 12 percent had reported its use in conjunction with another method.

We have noted that those methods closest to no method are most likely to be eventually reported as "no method." It is possible that the forgetting of these methods over time is related to failure in their use. The result of such selective attrition of failures would be an upward bias in the reported effectiveness of these methods. Indeed, 43 percent of the couples reporting second interval use of contraception at the first but not at the third interview reported failure of use at the first interview, while 32 percent of the couples reporting use at both interviews, reported failure.

[5] This fact means that inclusion of some contraceptors in the category "non-use" (discussed earlier) is not as problematic as it would be if the erroneously classified contraceptors used more effective methods.

Table 55. Reliability of reporting methods of contraception used in second birth interval: comparison between first and third interviews

First interview method	Second interview use of same method[a]	Use of same method	Over-lap	Different method	No Method	Total	Number of users
			Third interview report				
Total	58	48	27	14	11	100	655
Diaphragm and jelly	74	67	16	12	5	100	120
Condom	70	59	22	12	7	100	197
Withdrawal	40	26	21	32	21	100	34
Douche	23	8	24	48	20	100	25
Other	58	48	13	22	17	100	23
Rhythm	63	58	11	14	17	100	133
Rhythm combinations	31	17	64	12	7	100	42
Other combinations		14	73	4	10	100	81

[a] The Third Child, p. 268

Circumstances of Conception

Women who reported that they had used contraception before a given pregnancy were asked under what circumstances that pregnancy occurred and were handed a card which read:

(1) While we were actually using some method and didn't want a pregnancy just then.

(2) When we took a chance and didn't use a method.

(3) After we deliberately stopped using a method in order to have a child.

(4) Some other circumstance (Specify).

Virtually all responses fall in the first three categories, so we may ignore Category 4. For couples who reported at both the first and third interviews that they had used contraception in the second birth interval, there was general aggregate stability over the study period in the responses to this question as a result of counterbalancing discrepancies on the part of 23 percent of the sample (Table 56). Our primary interest in this question is to distinguish planned from unplanned pregnancies among women who had used contraception. Categories 1 and 2 are defined as unplanned and Category 3 as planned, and this distinction appears fairly reliable. There is, however, very poor consistency of reporting a failure while using as opposed to a failure from neglecting to use contraception. Of those reporting these two outcomes at both interviews, one-third are inconsistently reported. Perhaps we should ignore this distinction in future studies. In addition to problems of memory, it is not clear that a meaningful distinction is possible for methods such as rhythm and withdrawal. When does one fail and when does one "take a chance" with these methods?

If a woman reported that she had not used contraception before a given pregnancy, that pregnancy was considered as unplanned unless she gave as the only reason for not using contraception either that a child was wanted

Table 56. Consistency in reporting circumstances of conception leading to second birth for wives reporting consistently that contraception was used in second birth interval: comparison between first and third interviews

Circumstance reported in first interview	Circumstance reported in third interview			
	Using	Chance	Interrupted	Total
Total	18.5	14.4	67.1	100.0 (578)
While using a method	9.2	3.3	2.9	15.4
Taking a chance	5.5	7.8	4.2	17.5
Deliberately interrupted use	3.8	3.3	60.0	67.1

as soon as possible, or that there was anticipated difficulty in conceiving.

Is there any tendency over time for unplanned pregnancies to be remembered as planned? Table 57 cross-tabulates the pattern of consistency in reporting use of contraception by the pattern of consistency in reporting planning status. There is no trend over time toward the reporting of unplanned pregnancies as planned among women who report use of contraception either at both or at only one of the interviews, although women who inconsistently reported use of contraception were also highly likely to be inconsistently classified with respect to planning status. However, among women who reported non-use at both interviews, there is a marked tendency for pregnancies originally classified as unplanned to be classified as planned on the basis of data collected 8 years later. Among these women, 53 percent of the pregnancies classified as planned on the basis of the third interview data are classi-

141

Table 57. Consistency in classification of planning by consistency in reporting of contraceptive use for second birth interval: comparison between first and third interviews

Contraceptive use	Planning classification					
	Planned: both	Planned: first, not third	Planned: third, not first	Unplanned: both	Total	N
Use: both	59.2	8.2	6.5	26.1	100	586
Use: first, not third	45.9	13.1	9.8	31.2	100	61
Use: third, not first	20.9	25.4	20.9	32.8	100	67
Non-use: both	33.8	2.6	37.6	26.0	100	77

fied as unplanned on the basis of the first interview reports. So the classification of planning status for noncontraceptors, in addition to being highly unreliable, is also markedly biased over time in the direction of the "planned" classification. This may be of particular concern with respect to the planning classification of first pregnancies, since a substantial proportion of the population does not use contraception in the first interval and because this interval is the furthest removed in time from the date of interview.

Conception Time

Women who reported that they had used contraception and had deliberately interrupted its use in order to conceive were asked: "To the best of your memory, how many months was it before you became pregnant for the ——th

142

time?" We are able to compare second and third interview responses to this question for 104 women who reported a third pregnancy by the second interview and who reported at both interviews that contraception was deliberately interrupted in order to conceive. In almost two-thirds of these cases the two reports are within one month of each other (Table 58). However the two reports differ by as

Table 58. Consistency in reporting conception time for women who reported at both the second and the third interviews that they deliberately interrupted contraception before their third pregnancy.

Reported months before conception after interruption of contraception	N	Percent
Total	104	100.0
Same at both interviews	41	39.4
Reports differ by one month	27	26.0
Reports differ by two months	18	17.3
Reports differ by three months or more	18	17.3

much as 3 months or more for one-sixth of the cases. Since this variable is generally employed as a dependent variable (or as a component of a dependent variable) such individual instability is not serious in light of overall aggregate stability—mean waiting time is 3.1 and 3.5 months at the first and third interviews respectively. On the other hand, classifications (such as fecundity) based on retrospective reports of waiting time may misclassify a significant proportion of the sample.

143

Indices of Family-Planning Success

In fertility studies an index of family-planning success is often constructed to summarize the number and pattern of the planned and unplanned pregnancies that a couple has experienced. Two such indices are evaluated here: family-planning success as classified from the first and the third interviews.

Four levels of planning success were distinguished at the first interview: "completely planned" denotes that all pregnancies prior to the second birth were planned; couples classified as "semi-planned" had planned their last but not an earlier pregnancy; "completely unplanned" denotes that no pregnancies prior to the second birth were planned; and the remainder, mostly couples who planned their first but not their last pregnancy, were classified as "semi-unplanned."

This index was constructed again on the basis of the third-interview reports about pregnancies preceding the second birth, and the relationship between the first and third interview classifications is presented in Table 59. Although the time interval between the first and third interviews was on the average 5 years longer than the interval between the first and second interviews, the results in Table 59 are almost identical to those of a comparison between the first two interviews.[6] The proportion in each planning category is virtually the same independent of which interview serves as source of data. Comparing the first and third interview reports, the classifications are identical for 63 percent of the couples; for 5 percent they are in extreme disagreement (for the comparison between the first and second interview reports, the corresponding estimates were 64 and 6 percent respectively). Apparently there is a certain amount of error in these indices that is not affected by the time interval elapsing between reports. A comparison between religious groups in the degree of consistency on this index indicates that cases of extreme

[6] Westoff, Potter, and Sagi, *The Third Child*, p. 272.

144

Table 59. Consistency in the classification of fertility-planning success for pregnancies preceding the second birth

Success reported at first interview	Success reported at third interview				
	Completely planned	Semi-planned	Semi-unplanned	Completely unplanned	Total
Completely planned	33.4	5.0	4.2	1.5	44.1
Semi-planned	5.4	8.3	1.3	3.0	18.0
Semi-unplanned	3.0	0.9	8.3	3.2	15.4
Completely unplanned	3.8	2.3	3.3	13.1	22.5
Total	45.6	16.4	17.1	20.9	100.0

disagreement are disproportionately concentrated among Catholics (Table 60). The results are again similar whether the comparison is between the first and second or first and third interview classifications. As noted in *The Third Child*, this suggests that much of the extreme disagreement results from the reporting of reasons for not using contraception—such reasons serve as the basis of classification more for Catholics than for non-Catholics.[7] An analysis of cases classified in extreme disagreement (all pregnancies reported as planned at one interview but as unplanned at the other) reveals that the operational distinction between "planning" and "non-planning" reasons for not using contraception is not particularly salient to the respondents, and especially not so for Catholic women. For many Catholic women, "It's up to God" and "We want as many children as possible" are interchangeable statements.

An index of family-planning success has been constructed

[7] *Loc. cit.*

145

Table 60. Consistency in the classification of family-planning success
for pregnancies preceding the second birth, by religion

| Religion | Number | Degree of consistency | | | Total |
		Identical agreement	Extreme disagreement	Other disagreement	
		Comparison between first and second interview classifications [a]			
Protestant	372	66.2	2.2	31.6	100
Catholic	423	57.7	9.5	32.8	100
Jewish	110	79.1	5.4	15.5	100
Total	905	63.7	6.0	30.3	100
		Comparison between first and third interview classifications			
Protestant	331	68.9	3.3	27.8	100
Catholic	358	52.8	8.1	39.1	100
Jewish	96	81.2	2.1	16.7	100
Total	785[b]	63.0	5.4	31.6	100

[a] Westoff, Potter, and Sagi, The Third Child, Table C-7

[b] A third interview classification of first interview planning
status was not constructed for cases reporting at the third
interview that they had never used contraception since we
have for these cases only their current reason for non-use.

which summarizes a respondent's experience with all pregnancies up to the time of the third interview (for most women through the end of childbearing). In order to improve the validity of this measure, the planning status of each pregnancy was classified on the basis of the interview that most immediately followed that pregnancy in time. Most sample surveys have to rely on retrospective reports collected at one point in time. By comparing the index of family-planning success as constructed above to the index as constructed solely on the basis of third interview reports, we can assess the extent of misclassification inherent in the usual (and necessary) procedure. The patterns in Table 61 for all pregnancies are very similar to those observed in Tables 59 and 60 for pregnancies before the second birth. There is only a slight bias in the third interview data toward the reporting of all pregnancies as planned (30 as opposed to 27 percent). For almost two-thirds of the couples the two classifications are identical, and for only 2 percent is there extreme disagreement between the two measures. Whether or not these results are reassuring depends upon the purposes for which the variable is intended. As a dependent variable there is little bias imposed by using family-planning success as classified at one point in time. However, it is also a frequent practice to employ this variable as a control variable, examining relationships that obtain within categories of family-planning success. Of those classified solely on third interview data as "all pregnancies planned," 26 percent would not have been so classified on the basis of data collected at points nearer in time to the events in question; 39 percent of those classified as "all pregnancies unplanned" would not have been so classified. While these categories of family-planning success distinguish average ability to control fertility, they only crudely differentiate "types" of family planners.

Retrospective Report on Number of Children Desired after the Second Birth

Because family-size desires change over time, it is often important that we know how many children a respondent

147

Table 61. Index of family-planning success for all pregnancies based wholly on third interview data compared to the same index based on reports closest to events

Index based on reports closest to events	Index based wholly on third interview reports					
	All pregnancies planned	Majority planned	Half planned	Majority unplanned	All pregnancies unplanned	Total
All pregnancies planned	22.0	2.5	1.3	0.5	0.5	26.8
Majority planned	3.0	12.6	1.4	3.0	0.2	20.4
Half planned	2.0	1.0	6.2	2.3	1.1	12.7
Majority unplanned	1.4	3.4	1.8	11.6	4.6	22.8
All pregnancies unplanned	1.4	0.8	1.0	3.9	10.2	17.3
Total	29.9	20.4	11.7	21.4	16.7	100.0 (785)

wanted at times in the past as well as the number desired at the time of the interview. (See Chapter II for an analysis of the stability over time of this variable and of related questions of reliability.) The data reported here provide a unique opportunity to assess the reliability of such retrospective reports and to evaluate whether unreliability is related to intervening fertility. Respondents were asked at the first interview (6 months after second birth) how many children they desired. Approximately 8 years later, they were asked at the third interview how many children they had desired after the birth of their second child.

Slightly over half of the respondents accurately recalled the number of children they had desired 8 years earlier; for 14 percent of the women the two reports differed by more than one child. There is a clear tendency for the desired family size recalled to be higher than the number stated as desired at the first interview. Does intervening fertility affect the number that a woman remembers as originally desired? Table 62 presents clear evidence that it does. The original desires are most likely to be accurately recalled if a woman's completed family size is the same as those original desires; they are least accurately recalled among women who achieved smaller families than those desired after the second birth. The differences are very substantial: the two reports were identical for 73 percent of the former group but for only 32 percent of the latter group. Moreover, the direction of the discrepancy is strongly related to whether a woman exceeded, exactly achieved, or did not achieve her originally stated desires. Women who exceeded their original desires are much more likely to recall those desires as higher than their first interview report. Among women who achieved their original desires, approximately equal proportions recall family-size desires higher and lower than the first interview report. But the majority of the women who had fewer children than the number preferred at the first interview, recall those original desires as lower than they were. Women

149

Table 62. Third interview recall of family-size desires at first interview, by achievement of first interview desired family size and by planning of last pregnancy

	Third interview recall of first interview family-size desires				Number of women
	Higher	Same	Lower	Total	
Total	27	56	17	100	792
Achieved number of children relative to that desired at first interview					
Larger	34	57	9	100	235
Same	12	73	15	100	323
Smaller	7	32	61	100	234
Planning of last pregnancy					
Planned	24	60	16	100	379
Unplanned	30	52	18	100	413

tend to perceive their family-size desires at an earlier point in time as having been consistent with the number of children they ultimately achieve, whether or not this was the case.

Correlates of Unreliability

Unreliability in the reporting of fertility behavior would be least problematic if it were randomly distributed. Unfortunately, it is not. For purposes of comparison we have classified as "reliably reporting" those women who at the third interview gave a report consistent with their first interview report with respect both to the use of contraception and to the planning status of the first two pregnancies. As Table 63 illustrates, the proportion reliably reporting

150

Table 63. Percent reliably reporting both the use and non-use of contraception and the planning status of the first two pregnancies, by selected characteristics

Characteristics	Total number	Percent reliably reporting
Total	814	46
Wife's education		
Under 12 years	153	37
12 years	428	43
College	233	58
Religion		
Protestant	333	55
Catholic	383	32
Jewish	98	71
Family-planning success to third interview		
All planned	221	71
Majority planned	161	44
Half planned	103	33
Majority unplanned	182	31
All unplanned	146	39
Number of pregnancies between first and third interviews		
0	198	61
1	256	48
2	183	43
3+	177	30

these events varies with education, religion, family-planning success, and the number of pregnancies intervening between the two reports. The religious difference is particularly striking with 71 percent of the Jews but 32 percent of the Catholics classified as reliably reporting. At

151

first it appeared that the relationship of reliability to the number of intervening pregnancies might in large part explain the other relationships observed here. It is reasonable that the difficulty of accurately recalling events surrounding the first two pregnancies would increase with the number of pregnancies that have since occurred. Consequently we would expect the highest fertility subgroups to be the least reliable in reporting about early pregnancies. However, a multivariate analysis indicates that when the number of pregnancies is controlled, the effect of family-planning status on reliability is reduced by about one-third, and the effects of education and religion are reduced only slightly. Most of the remaining relationships are most probably attributable to differences in the use of contraception and consequently to differences in the extent to which planning status is classified on the basis of the highly unreliable "reasons for not using contraception."

Effect of Reliability on Measured Correlations

The unreliability we have found in retrospective reports of fertility and surrounding circumstances is not surprising. It would be unrealistic to expect that women would recall accurately circumstances surrounding events that occurred many years earlier and that were not necessarily salient to them even then. Nevertheless, unreliability of reporting may depress our measured associations between these early variables and others. We can evaluate this issue with respect to the index of family-planning success in two ways: by comparing the correlations obtained when this variable is based on earlier rather than later data, and by comparing the correlations obtained among women who reported "reliably" with those among women reporting "unreliably."

Correlations between the index of family-planning success and fertility variables are only slightly decreased by basing this index solely on third interview data instead of on the data collected nearer the events in question (Table 64). For example, completed family-size correlates .21 with the index of family-planning success before the second

Table 64. Correlations between the indices of family-planning success and selected variables

Index of family-planning success	Age of wife	Interval marriage to second birth	Number of children desired at second birth	Completed family size	Number of women
First interview classification:					
Based on first interview					
Total	-.17	-.35	.21	.21	814
Third interview report consistent with first	-.27	-.46	.23	.25	495
Third interview report inconsistent with first	-.02	-.17	.15	.11	319
Based on third interview	-.26	-.35	.16	.18	814
Third interview classification:					
Based on closest interviews	-.20	-.36	.21	.31	814
Based only on third interview	-.25	-.38	.17	.27	814

child as based on first interview data, but .18 with this variable as based on third interview data. Similarly the third interview index correlates .31 with completed fertility when based on data from the closest interviews as compared to a correlation of .27 when the index is constructed from the third interview alone. (That the correlation between family-planning success and age is higher when based on the later data reflects the tendency of older women to report pregnancies as "planned" which were previously reported as "unplanned.")

While only slight gains are made by basing these indices on the earliest possible data, it is clear that the correlations are considerably higher among women who are classified "consistent." Although women who report consistently the circumstances of their first two pregnancies are likely to be more reliable on other measures as well, some unreliability undoubtedly remains in these other measures so that the effect of reliability demonstrated here is not a maximal estimate. Nevertheless, the correlations between the planning of the first two births and both the average birth interval and completed family size are over twice as high for women reporting consistently as they are for women reporting inconsistently. However, only the correlations with age and average birth interval are substantially higher for those reporting consistently than for the total sample.

Summary

In summary, there is a great deal of unreliability in most of the retrospective reports of fertility and fertility-related variables examined here. Certain variables or types of analyses (such as distinctions between types of contraceptive failure or analyses among noncontraceptors) are called into question by these data on reliability. While most variables are sufficiently reliable for their use to be justified, it is likely that our measures of association are often depressed by unreliability of measurement. Surely, an important concern of future fertility research must be to improve the reliability with which the basic fertility variables are measured.

154

Epilogue

At the completion of the Princeton Fertility Study, the major example of longitudinal research on American fertility to date, we would do well to reflect briefly on the value of such studies and on the lessons learned about their design and execution.

It seems clear that many questions of major importance to our understanding of the dynamics of fertility cannot be approached nearly as well any other way. One advantage of considerable importance is that a longitudinal design permits assessing the extent to which fertility is guided by the desires of the parents, that is, the ability of couples to achieve a particular goal. It is obviously essential to such assessment that the number of children desired is measured before the event of the fertility it is intended to predict; only with prior measurement can we have confidence that such desires are not contaminated by the behavior we wish to predict. This is as important for the analysis of variables for which we report negative findings (for example, personality characteristics and mobility aspirations) as it is for the analyses in which predictive relationships were uncovered (for example, the effect of the number of children wanted on the efficacy of contraceptive use and the timing and number of births). It is particularly critical for understanding the dynamics of relationships in which the variables interact with each other over time such as the connections between fertility and the wife's work history (a problem requiring even more frequent re-interviews than were made in our study).

Another advantage of the longitudinal design is the opportunity it affords to evaluate the stability of family-size desires. It is obvious that couples vary in the degree to which they have specific numbers in mind; they also differ in the variability of this attitude over time. Our research design permits some assessment of the stability of family-size desires over an extended period of time.

One feature of longitudinal studies that cannot be

planned in advance is the occasional, quite fortuitous, experimental opportunities provided by changes in the society at large. The Princeton Fertility Study was the beneficiary of two such events—an economic recession and the introduction of the oral contraceptive. The economic recession of 1957-58 occurred between our first and second interviews and gave us an opportunity to assess its effects on the fertility of those people affected. The pill emerged between our second and third interviews and gave us, quite accidentally, the only good data of its kind—with a before and after measurement—on the association between the pill and coital frequency. Obviously, one cannot count on the occurrence of such natural experiments but a longitudinal study does permit the exploitation of such opportunities if they arise.

The longitudinal design also offers methodological payoffs both in minimizing recall error through collecting information at points in time close to the events in question, and in providing repeated opportunities to assess the reliability of retrospective reports on fertility and fertility control. It seems clear that questions asked about such matters as methods of contraception used, miscarriages, and other factual details will be more reliably reported when the events in question are not too distant from the interview. Thus, longitudinal studies not only permit prospective reports, they also enhance the quality of data collected by retrospective questions. Moreover, since such designs by definition involve more than one interview with the same respondents, there is an opportunity to assess the reliability of such interview data by repeating the same questions about the same events and examining the consistency of response. In this study we were able to measure such reliability at two intervals: 3 years and 6 to 10 years. One of the important questions examined was whether there is any relationship between the length of recall and a tendency to report pregnancies as planned which were reported originally as unintentional. Similar analyses were conducted on the reliability of reporting whether contraception was used in a particular pregnancy interval and the specific methods of contraception used.

Several methodological lessons were learned in the course of this study. The difficulty experienced in locating respondents at the second interview suggests the desirability of contacting respondents annually—a procedure followed with great success at the third interview. The practice of phasing the last interviews over a number of years, although it looked very reasonable at the time, caused many problems. Designed to maximize simultaneously interview completion rates and the extent of completed fertility, the result of spreading the interviews over five years created more problems for the analysis of time-related variables than it solved.

A more fundamental methodological problem of the research design arose from the parity-specific nature of the sample. Discussed at some length in Chapter VI, the main problem in our case was the difficulty introduced in analyses in which the length of time to the second and subsequent births is involved with other variables, particularly those socioeconomic characteristics associated with time and the life cycle. Parity-specific samples are appropriate for only limited types of analyses and great caution should be exercised in the future choice of such samples.

There is little question that the considerable cost of longitudinal studies is justified by their payoff. Our conviction on this point is strong enough to encourage us to undertake another longitudinal study (as part of the 1970 National Fertility Study planned with Norman B. Ryder) in which we hope to exploit the experience gained in the Princeton Fertility Study.

Appendix A
Statistical Significance

In general, tests for statistical significance are inappropriate for the kinds of analyses reported in this volume. Confidence in the conclusions reached must be derived from the extent to which they corroborate findings based on other bodies of data or, when new directions are suggested, from the support (or lack of it) of future analyses. The following table is provided only as an indication of the size of relationships that would be required to satisfy statistical significance under the assumptions of the t test for the significance of a correlation.

Table A-1. Coefficients of correlation required to reject the hypothesis p = 0 at 5 and 1 percent levels of significance

| | Magnitude of r's by levels of significance | | Degrees of freedom (N-2) |
	5%	1%	
Total sample	.07	.10	812
Protestant	.11	.15	331
Active	.17	.22	134
Other	.14	.19	195
Catholic	.10	.14	381
Active	.20	.26	93
Other	.12	.16	286
Jewish	.20	.26	96

159

APPENDIX B

Related Publications

The following is a complete list of articles and papers relating to the plans for the study, preliminary substantive reports, and analyses of other subjects based on study data.

Clyde V. Kiser, "Exploration of Possibilities for New Studies of Factors Affecting Size of Family," *Milbank Memorial Fund Quarterly* 31 (1953): 436-80.

Charles F. Westoff, Elliot G. Mishler, Robert G. Potter, Jr., and Clyde V. Kiser, "A New Study of American Fertility: Social and Psychological Factors," *Eugenics Quarterly* 2 (1955): 229-33.

Clyde V. Kiser, "General Objectives and Broad Areas of Interest in a Proposed New Study in Fertility," *Current Research in Human Fertility*, Milbank Memorial Fund (New York, 1955), pp. 115-20.

Elliot G. Mishler, and Charles F. Westoff, "A Proposal for Research on Social Psychological Factors Affecting Fertility: Concepts and Hypotheses," *ibid.*, pp. 121-50.

Philip M. Hauser, "Some Observations on Method and Study Design," *ibid.*, pp. 151-62.

Clyde V. Kiser, Elliot G. Mishler, Charles F. Westoff, and Robert G. Potter, Jr., "Development of Plans for a Social Psychological Study of the Future Fertility of Two-Child Families," *Population Studies* 10 (1956): 43-52.

Elliot G. Mishler, "A Scalogram Analysis of the Sentence Completion Test," *Educational and Psychological Measurement* 18 (1958): 75-90.

Robert G. Potter, Jr., "An Analysis of Birth-Spacing Preferences," paper presented at the 1958 Meetings of the Population Association of America; abstracted in *Population Index* 24 (1958): 213.

Frank W. Notestein, Elliot G. Mishler, Robert G. Potter, Jr., and Charles F. Westoff, "Pretest Results of a New

160

Study of Fertility in the United States," *International Statistical Institute Bulletin* 36 (1959): 154-64.

Robert G. Potter, Jr., "Contraceptive Practice and Birth Intervals among Two-Child White Couples in Metropolitan America," *Thirty Years of Research in Human Fertility: Retrospect and Prospect*, Proceedings of a Round Table at the 1958 Annual Conference, Milbank Memorial Fund (New York), pp. 74-92.

Philip C. Sagi, "A Component Analysis of Birth Intervals among Two-Child White Couples in Metropolitan America," *ibid.*, pp. 135-48.

Charles F. Westoff, "Religion and Fertility in Metropolitan America," *ibid.*, pp. 117-34.

Philip C. Sagi, "Interim Report on the Study of Future Fertility of Two-Child Families in Metropolitan America," paper presented at the annual meetings of the American Statistical Association in Chicago, December 1958; published in the 1958 *Proceedings* of the Social Statistics Section, 1959.

Charles F. Westoff, "The Social-Psychological Structure of Fertility," paper presented at the meeting of the International Union for the Scientific Study of Population (Vienna, 1959); published in the *Proceedings*.

Clyde V. Kiser, "Fertility Rates by Residence and Migration," *ibid.*

Charles F. Westoff, Marvin Bressler, and Philip C. Sagi, "The Concept of Social Mobility: An Empirical Inquiry," *American Sociological Review* 25 (1960): 375-85.

Robert G. Potter, Jr., "Length of the Observation Period as a Factor Affecting the Contraceptive Failure Rate," *Milbank Memorial Fund Quarterly* 38 (April, 1960): 140-52.

Robert G. Potter, Jr., "Some Comments on the Evidence Pertaining to Family Limitation in the United States," *Population Studies* 14, No. 1 (July, 1960).

Robert G. Potter, Jr., "Some Relationships between Short Range and Long Range Risks of Unwanted Pregnancy," *Milbank Memorial Fund Quarterly* 38, No. 3 (July, 1960): 255-63.

161

Charles F. Westoff, "The 'Family Growth in Metropolitan America' Study: A Progress Report," paper presented at the Conference on Family Planning jointly sponsored by The Milbank Memorial Fund and The Population Council (October, 1960); to be published in the Proceedings of the Conference.

Robert G. Potter, Jr., and Philip C. Sagi, "Some Procedure for Estimating the Sampling Fluctuations of a Contraceptive Failure Rate," *ibid.*

Charles F. Westoff, Robert G. Potter, Jr., and Philip C. Sagi, "Some Estimates of the Reliability of Survey Data on Family Planning," *Population Studies* 15, No. 1 (July, 1961): 32-69.

Robert G. Potter, Jr., Philip C. Sagi, and Charles F. Westoff, "Knowledge of the Ovulatory Cycle and Coital Frequency as Factors Affecting Conception and Contraception," *Milbank Memorial Fund Quarterly* 40 (Jan., 1962): 46-58.

Robert G. Potter, Jr., Philip C. Sagi, and Charles F. Westoff, "Some Neglected Factors Pertaining to Fertility Control," *Fertility and Sterility* 13, No. 3 (May-June, 1962): 259-64.

Robert G. Potter, Jr., Philip C. Sagi, and Charles F. Westoff, "Improvement of Contraception during the Course of Marriage," *Population Studies* (Nov., 1962) 160-74.

Philip C. Sagi and Charles F. Westoff, "An Exercise in Partitioning Some Components of the Variance of Family Size," *Emerging Techniques in Population Research*, Proceedings of the 1962 Annual Conference of the Milbank Memorial Fund (New York, 1963), pp. 130-40.

Charles F. Westoff, Robert G. Potter, Jr., and Philip C. Sagi, "Some Selected Findings of the Princeton Fertility Study: 1963," *Demography* 1, No. 1 (1964): 130-35.

Robert G. Potter, Jr., "Application of Life Table Techniques to Measurement of Contraceptive Effectiveness," *Demography* 3, No. 2 (1966): 297-304.

David L. Featherman, "The Socioeconomic Achievement of

White Married Males in the United States, 1957-67," Ph.D. dissertation, University of Michigan, 1969.

Charles F. Westoff, Larry Bumpass, and Norman B. Ryder, "Oral Contraception, Coital Frequency and Time Required to Conceive," *Social Biology* 16, No. 1 (1969): 1-10.

Larry Bumpass and Charles F. Westoff, "The Prediction of Completed Fertility," *Demography* 6, No. 4 (1969): 445-54.

AUTHOR INDEX

Akers, D. S., 41

Berent, J., 89
Blau, P. M., 104, 105, 106, 112, 113, 118, 129
Bumpass, L. L., 5, 24, 25, 39, 41, 44, 45, 70, 77, 79, 94

Campbell, A. A., 4, 36, 55, 77, 79
Coble, J. M., 89
Coombs, L., 5, 24, 25, 41, 44

Dumont, A., 104
Duncan, B., 111, 125, 129
Duncan, O. D., 89, 90, 93, 104, 105, 106, 111, 112, 113, 118, 125, 129

Featherman, D. L., 18, 104ff, 106, 108, 111, 113, 115, 122, 125, 128, 129
Freedman, R., 4, 5, 24, 25, 41, 44, 55, 77, 79, 89, 94
Friedman, J., 5

Goldberg, D., 74, 77
Gordon, R. A., 51

Heise, D. R., 25, 27
Henry, L., 69
Hodge, R. W., 118

Kantner, J. F., 86, 89
Kelly, E. L., 41, 44
Kiser, C. V., 5, 74

Mishler, E. G., 3, 9, 41, 44, 92, 96, 105, 136
Moberg, S., 89

Patterson, J. E., 4, 36, 55, 77, 79
Potter, R. G., Jr., 3, 9, 32, 55, 62, 77, 86, 89, 92, 93, 96, 105, 133, 136, 144, 146

Ridley, J. C., 74
Ryder, N. B., 4, 24, 41, 55, 70, 79, 82, 132, 157

Sagi, P. C., 3, 9, 32, 55, 77, 92, 93, 96, 105, 133, 136, 144, 146
Sheps, M. C., 74
Siegel, J. S., 41
Slesinger, D. P., 89
Svalastoga, K., 112
Sweet, J. A., 95

Westoff, C. F., 3, 9, 24, 32, 39, 41, 44, 45, 55, 70, 74, 77, 79, 82, 90, 92, 93, 96, 105, 132, 133, 136, 144, 146
Whelpton, P. K., 4, 5, 36, 55, 77, 79